Avot

D'Rabbi Natan

Rabbi
Natan H'Babli

SimchatChaim.com

There is no known book without mistakes. Therefore, I ask in every language of application if anyone has any questions, comments, clarifications, corrections, please send to: simchatchaim@yahoo.com

All material used in this section may not be used for commercial purposes, but only for study and teaching.

To get this book or books and information Email me at:

simchatchaim@yahoo.com

Copyright©All Rights Reserved to

www.simchatchaim.com

Itzhak Hoki Aboudi ©All rights reserved to the Editor

מהדורה שניה תשפ"ד
Second edition 2024

Avot D'Rabbi Natan - The contents of the book

The contents of the book

Page	Chapter
3.	Introduction to the book
5.	Chapter 1
19.	Chapter 2
31.	Chapter 3
37.	Chapter 4
44.	Chapter 5
45.	Chapter 6
52.	Chapter 7
55.	Chapter 8
60.	Chapter 9
66.	Chapter 10
68.	Chapter 11
73.	Chapter 12
83.	Chapter 13
85.	Chapter 14
90.	Chapter 15
95.	Chapter 16
100.	Chapter 17
104.	Chapter 18
107.	Chapter 19
109.	Chapter 20
112.	Chapter 21
114.	Chapter 22
116.	Chapter 23
119.	Chapter 24
122.	Chapter 25

Avot D'Rabbi Natan - The contents of the book

128.	Chapter 26
131.	Chapter 27
134.	Chapter 28
137.	Chapter 29
142.	Chapter 30
145.	Chapter 31
149.	Chapter 32
152.	Chapter 33
157.	Chapter 34
164.	Chapter 35
169.	Chapter 36
174.	Chapter 37
180.	Chapter 38
184.	Chapter 39
186.	Chapter 40
192.	Chapter 41

Avot D'Rabbi Natan - introduction

Introduction to the book

Avot de-Rabbi Nathan [Jewish Babylonian Aramaic: אבות דרבי נתן], usually printed together with the minor tractates of the Talmud, is a Jewish Aggadic work probably compiled in the geonic era (c.700–900 CE). Although Avot de-Rabbi Nathan is the first and longest of the **minor tractates**, it probably does not belong in that collection chronologically, having more the character of a late midrash. In the form now extant it contains a mixture of Mishnah and Midrash, and may be technically designated as a homiletical exposition of the Mishnaic tractate **Pirkei Avot**, having for its foundation an older recension version of that tractate. It may be considered as a kind of **Tosefta** or **Talmud** to the Mishna Avot, which does not possess a traditional Talmud. Avot de-Rabbi Nathan contains many teachings, proverbs, and incidents that are not found anywhere else in the early rabbinical literature. Other rabbinical sayings appear in a more informal style than what is found in Pirkei Avot.

The content of the two recensions differs considerably, although the method is the same in both. The separate teachings of the Mishnah Avot are generally taken as texts, which are either briefly explained - the ethical lessons contained therein being supported by reference to Biblical passages - or fully illustrated by narratives and legends. Sometimes long digressions are made by introducing subjects connected only loosely with the text. The following example may illustrate this method: Commenting on the teaching of Simon the Just which

Avot D'Rabbi Natan - introduction

designates charity as one of the three pillars on which the world rests, Avot de-Rabbi Nathan reads as follows:

How does the world rest on charity? Behold, the prophet said - in the name of the Lord, I desired charity mercy, and not sacrifice. The world was created only by charity [mercy], as is said, Mercy shall be built up forever. or, as the rabbis translate this passage, The world is built on mercy. Rabbi Yochanan ben Zakai, accompanied by Rabbi Yehoshua once passed Jerusalem after its fall. While looking upon the city and the ruins of the Temple, R. Joshua exclaimed, 'Woe unto us, that the holy place is destroyed which atoned for our sins!' R. Yochanan replied, 'My son, do not grieve on this account, for we have another atonement for our sins; it is charity, as is said, I desired charity and not sacrifice.

Avot D'Rabbi Natan - Chapter 1

Chapter 1

Moses was sanctified in a cloud, and received Torah from Sinai. As it says, "And the glory of the Eternal dwelt on Mount Sinai"; that was for Moses, in order to purify him. This was after the giving of the Ten Commandments, according to Rabbi Yosei HaGalili. But Rabbi Akiva says as the verse continues, "and the cloud covered it for six days" – that was for Moses; and only then, "On the seventh day He called to Moses from within the cloud," in order give honor to Moses. Rabbi Natan said: And why was Moses held back for those six days, without God's speech resting upon him? So that he could be emptied of all the food and drink that was in his stomach, so that when he was sanctified, he would be like the angels who serve God. Rabbi Matya ben Heresh said to him: Master, they told him this only to terrify him, so that he would receive the words of Torah with terror and awe, trembling and sweating, as it says, "Serve the Eternal with awe, and rejoice with trembling."

Once it happened that Rabbi Yoshiah and Rabbi Matya ben Heresh were both sitting and engaging in words of Torah. Rabbi Yoshiah began to leave, to go to work to the "way of the world". Rabbi Matya ben Heresh said to him: How can you abandon the words of the living God and immerse yourself in the way of the world? Even though you are my master and I am your student, I still must say that it is not good to abandon the words of the living God and immerse in the way of the world! So, it was said about them: Whenever they would sit and engage in Torah, they would zealously argue with one another, but when they parted, they did so as if they were young lovers.

Avot D'Rabbi Natan - Chapter 1

The Torah was given at Sinai through Moses' hands, as it says, "He wrote them on two stone tablets, and He gave them to me." And then later it says, "These are the decrees and the laws and the teachings that the Eternal gave, through Moses on Mount Sinai, between Him and the children of Israel." The Torah that the Holy Blessed One gave to Israel was given only through Moses, as it says, "Between Me and the children of Israel"; Moses merited to be a messenger between the children of Israel and the Omnipresent God. Moses prepared the inaugural ram and the anointing oil, and anointed Aaron and his sons with it all seven days of inauguration and from it, all the high priests and kings are anointed. And Elazar burned the red heifer as a sin offering, with which impurities would be purified for generations. Rabbi Eliezer said: Great is this ritual, for it is practiced throughout the generations, just as Aaron and his sons were sanctified with this anointing oil, as it says, "Anoint Aaron and his sons, and sanctify them to serve as priests."

Joshua received from Moses – as it says, "Give him some of your majesty, so that the whole congregation of the children of Israel will heed him." The Elders received from Joshua – as it says, "The people served the Eternal all the days of Joshua and all the days of the Elders who lived on after Joshua and who had seen all the great works that the Eternal had performed for Israel." The Judges received from Joshua – as it says, "And it was in the days that the Judges judged." The early Prophets received it from the Judges – as it says, "And I sent you all my servants, the prophets, daily and persistently." Haggai, Zechariah, and Malachi received from the Prophets. The Men of the Great Assembly received from Haggai, Zechariah, and Malachi. And they said three things: Be

Avot D'Rabbi Natan - Chapter 1

deliberate in judgment, and raise up many students, and make a fence around the Torah.

Be deliberate in judgment. How so? This teaches that a person should carefully deliberate in judgment, for all who are careful in judgment will feel settled about their judgment, as it says, "These, too, are the proverbs of Solomon, which the men of King Hezekiah of Judah copied." This does not mean they merely copied them, but that they deliberated over them. Abba Shaul says: They did not merely deliberate carefully over them, but explained them. Originally, they would say: Proverbs, and Song of Songs, and Ecclesiastes had to be hidden, for people would recite proverbs that were at odds with Scripture. So, they decided to hide them, until the Men of the Great Assembly came along and explained them, as it says, "I saw among the simple, and noticed among the children, a youth with no sense……and behold a woman came up to him, dressed like a prostitute, with a guarded heart. She is restless and rebellious. Her legs are never at home. Sometimes she is outside, sometimes in the streets; she lurks on every corner. She grabs him, and kisses him, and boldly says to him: I made well-being sacrifices; today I fulfilled my vows. That is why I came up to you, seeking you, and have found you. I have draped my couch with covers of dyed Egyptian cloth. I have scented my bed with myrrh, aloes, and cinnamon. Let us go and fill ourselves with love until the morning. Let us indulge in loving. For the man of the house is out, he has gone on the road, far away. He took a bundle of money with him, and will not come back home until the full moon." And in Song of Songs it is written, "Let us go, my beloved, out into field. Let us spend the night in the villages. We will wake up in the vineyards, and see if the vines have

Avot D'Rabbi Natan - Chapter 1

flowered, if its blossoms have opened, and if the pomegranates are in bloom. There I will give my love to you." And in Ecclesiastes it is written, "Young man, enjoy your childhood! Let your heart feel good while you are still young! Follow the ways of your heart and the visions of your eyes. But know that for all these things, God will bring you to judgment." And it is written in Song of Songs, "I am my beloved's, and his desire is upon me." They did not merely deliberate over them, but explained them!

Another interpretation: Be deliberate in judgment. How so? This teaches that a person should carefully consider his words, and not be severe with his words, for one who is severe with his words forgets his words. For so we find with Moses our teacher, that when he was severe with his words, he forgot his words. Where do we find that Moses our teacher forgot his words? For it says, "Elazar the priest said to the troops who had come in from the war: This is the decree of the Torah that God has commanded Moses." He commanded Moses, and did not command me? He commanded Moses, my father's brother, and did not command me? And where do we find that Moses was severe with his words? For it says with regard to the commanders of the army that, "Moses became angry with the commanders of the army…and he said to them: You have let all the women live!" If so, then what do we learn from the phrase, "all the women" Rather, this is a reference to the advice that Bil'am the wicked gave regarding Israel, as it is written, "And now, as I go back to my people, and I will advise you as to what this people will do to your people at the end of days." He said to King Balak: This people that you hate, they are hungry for food and thirsty for drink, but they have nothing to eat or drink

Avot D'Rabbi Natan - Chapter 1

but manna alone. Go and set up tents, and put food and drink in them, and then place beautiful women inside – the daughters of kings – so that this people will be seduced into worshiping Ba'al Peor, and will fall into the hand of God. Immediately, Balak went and did everything Bil'am the wicked told him. And see what Bil'am the wicked caused to happen to Israel, for twenty-four thousand of them fell, as it says, "And those that died in the plague were twenty-four thousand." And if Moses our teacher, the greatest of all sages and the father of the prophets, forgot his own words when he became severe with his words, would it not be all the more so with us? This teaches that a person should always consider his words carefully, and not be severe with his words. Ben Azzai said: Be careful with your words, and do not use them wastefully.

And make a fence around the Torah. And make a fence around your words, the way the Holy Blessed One made a fence around His words and Adam made a fence around his words. The Torah made a fence around its words. Moses made a fence around his words. Even Job, and even the Prophets and the sages – they all made a fence around their words.

What is the fence that the Holy Blessed One made around His words? It says, "All the nations will say: Why has the Eternal done such a thing to this land?" This teaches you that it was well known to the One who spoke and brought the world into being, that future generations would say this. Therefore, the Holy Blessed One said to Moses: Moses! Write this and place it in the Torah for future generations: "Then they will be told, because they forsook the covenant of the Eternal…and they went and served other gods and bowed down before them, gods

Avot D'Rabbi Natan - Chapter 1

that they did not know, and were not meant for them." From here we learn that the Holy Blessed One made a fence around His words, and wrote after this what they would one day say. Because of this, He is able to take reward away from His creatures with no argument.

What is the fence that Adam made around his words? It says, "The Eternal God commanded Adam: From every tree of the garden, you may absolutely eat. But from the Tree of Knowledge of Good and Evil, do not eat. For on the day, you eat from it, you will surely die." Adam the first person did not want to tell Eve in same the way that the

Holy Blessed One had told him. Instead, he said this to her thus making a fence around his words, saying more than what the Holy Blessed One had said to him: God said not to eat from the tree that is in the midst of the garden, nor to touch it, lest you die. He wanted to keep himself and Eve from even touching the tree.

So, then the snake said to himself: Since I cannot make Adam stumble, I will make Eve stumble. He went and sat beside her, and began chatting with her, and said to her: If you say the Holy Blessed One commanded us not to touch it, look, I will touch it and I will not die. And even you, if you touch it, you will not die. What did the wicked snake do then? He went up and touched the tree with his hands and feet, and shook it until its fruits fell to the ground. Some say that he did not touch it at all, for when the tree saw him; it screamed and said to him, wicked one! Wicked one! Don't touch me! As it says, "Do not bring the foot of the arrogant upon me, nor let the hand of the wicked push me away."

Another interpretation of "Do not bring the foot of the arrogant upon me": This is Titus the wicked, whose bones

Avot D'Rabbi Natan - Chapter 1

would grind in the grave because he would raise his hands and then strike the altar with them, and say: Locus! Locus! Latin for "the Omnipresent God." You are a King, and I am a king! Come and make war with me! How many bulls have been slaughtered for you? How many birds' necks have been snapped for you? How much wine has been poured out for you? How much incense has been burnt for you? And yet, you are the one who destroys the whole world! As it says, "Oh Ariel, Ariel, the city where David camped" Through year after year, and the cycle of festivals I will assault Ariel, and there will be groaning and sighing."

Again, the snake spoke to her and said: If you say the Holy Blessed One commanded us not to eat from the tree, look, I will eat from it and I will not die. And even you, if you eat from it you will not die. What did Eve think to herself? Since everything my master has told me so far has been lies – for in the beginning, Eve called Adam "my master," so she took the fruit and ate it and gave it to Adam, and he ate, as it says, "The woman saw that the tree was good for eating, for it was tempting to the eyes." At that moment, Eve was cursed with ten curses, as it says, "He said to the woman: I will increase and increase your pangs in childbearing; you will give birth to children in pain. You will desire your husband, and he will rule over you." This "increase" and that "increase" – one refers to the blood from the pain of menstruation and one refers to the blood from the pain of virginity. "Pangs" refers to the pain of raising children, and "childbearing" refers to the pain of pregnancy. "You will give birth to children in pain" is exactly what it says. "You will desire your husband" teaches that the woman desires her husband when he leaves for a trip. "And he will rule over

Avot D'Rabbi Natan - Chapter 1

you" means that a man declares his will aloud, while a woman keeps hers silent. She is wrapped up as if she were in mourning, held captive as if she were in prison, and kept apart from all men. And what was it that caused her to touch the fruit? The fence that Adam made around his words! Because of this, they say: If a person makes a fence around his words, he will not be able to live up to his words. And they also say: A person should not add upon the words that he hears. Rabbi Yosei says: Better a fence ten handbreadths high that stands, than one that is a hundred arm-lengths high that falls!

What was the wicked snake thinking during that episode? I will go and kill Adam and marry his wife, and then I will be king of the whole world! And I will walk tall and upright, and I will eat all the delicacies of the world! So, the Holy Blessed One said to him: You said, I will kill Adam and marry Eve. Thus, "I will place hostility between you and the woman". You said, I will be king of the whole world. Thus, "you will be the most cursed of all the animals". You said, I will walk tall and upright. Thus, "you will crawl on your belly". You said, I will eat all the delicacies of the world. Thus, "you will eat dirt all the days of your life".

Rabbi Shimon ben Menasya said: It is a pity that a great helper was lost from the world. For if the snake had not been cursed, everyone in Israel, the Jewish people would have two snakes in his house. One would be sent out to the west, and one would be sent out to the east, and they would bring back gems and precious stones and pearls and every precious thing in the world. And no creature could harm them. Not only that, but they could put them underneath a camel, or a donkey, or a mule, and they

Avot D'Rabbi Natan - Chapter 1

would gather the dung and bring it to gardens and orchards for fertilizer.

Rabbi Yehudah ben Beteira says: Adam was sitting in the Garden of Eden, and the angels who serve God stood there in the Garden attending to him. They grilled meat for him, and chilled wine for him. The snake came and saw all this, and took it as an affront to his own honor, and he became jealous.

How was Adam created? In the first hour, his dirt was gathered together. In the second hour, his form was formed. In the third hour, a torso was made. In the fourth hour, his limbs were attached. In the fifth hour, his orifices were opened. In the sixth hour, he was given breath. In the seventh hour, he stood up on his legs. In the eighth hour, he was paired with Eve. In the ninth hour, he was brought into the Garden of Eden. In the tenth hour, he was commanded not to eat from the tree. In the eleventh hour, he disgraced himself. In the twelfth hour, he was driven out and left, which fulfills the words of the verse, "Man does not spend even one night in honor."

What is recited on the first day? "The earth is the Eternal's, in all its fullness; the world and those who dwell upon it". For He became Master of the World and will judge it. What is recited on the second day? "The Eternal is great and praised tremendously in the city of our God". For He sets up all His works and becomes everything over His world. What is recited on the third day? "God stands in the divine congregation; amidst the powers He judges". For He created the sea and the land, and the land was folded into its place, and a space was cleared for His congregation. What is recited on the fourth day? "God of Vengeance, Lord! God of Vengeance, appear!" For He created the sun and the

Avot D'Rabbi Natan - Chapter 1

moon and the stars and the constellations, and they illuminate the world, and will one day be paid for their work. What is recited on the fifth day? "Sing joyously to the Eternal, our strength, shouts out to the God of Jacob!" For He created birds and fish, and sea creatures, who all sing joyously in the world. What is recited on the sixth day? "The Eternal is king, He is dressed in dignity; the Eternal has dressed, and wrapped Himself in strength. The world is set in place; it will not fall". He finished all of His works, and then rose above them and sat up in the heights of the world. What is recited on the seventh day? "A psalm, a song for the Sabbath day". For on it, there is no eating or drinking, no buying or selling. The righteous just sit, with crowns on their heads, and bask in the radiance of the Divine Presence, as it says, "And they beheld God, and they ate and drank," like the angels who serve God.

And why was he created so close to the Sabbath? So that he could enter into the Sabbath meal immediately.

Rabbi Shimon ben Elazar says: I will give you a parable. What was Adam like? "Like a man who married a convert, and would sit with her and give her orders." He said to her: Girl, do not eat bread while your hands are impure. And do not eat fruit that has not been tithed. And do not desecrate the Sabbath. And do not break your vows. And do not go around with other men. Now, if you break any one of these rules, you will die. Then what did that man do? He ate bread in front of her while his hands were impure, and he ate fruit that had not been tithed, and he desecrated the Sabbath, and he broke his vows. And then he cast her out. What did this convert say to herself? All the rules that my husband ordered me to follow are lies! She immediately went and broke them all.

Avot D'Rabbi Natan - Chapter 1

Rabbi Shimon ben Yochai says: I will give you a parable. What was the situation with Adam like? Like a man who had a woman in his house. What did he do? He went and brought a jar and put figs and nuts in it. Then he caught a scorpion, and put it near the mouth of the jar. And then he sealed the jar with a string and placed it in a corner. He said to her: Girl, everything I have in this house is for you to use, except for that jar, which you must not touch at all. What did the woman do? When her husband went out to the marketplace, she went and opened the jar, and stuck her hand inside, and the scorpion bit her. She went and fell on the bed. When her husband came back from the marketplace, he said to her: What happened? She said to him: I stuck my hand in the jar, and a scorpion bit me, and now I am dying! He said to her: Didn't I tell you before? Everything I have in my house is for you to use, except for that jar, which you must not touch at all! He became very angry at her and cast her out. So, it was with Adam, When the Holy Blessed One said to him, "From every tree of the garden you may absolutely eat. But from the Tree of Knowledge of Good and Evil, do not eat. For on the day, you eat from it, you will surely die." Then when he ate from it, he was driven out, which fulfills the verse, "Man does not spend even one night in honor. He is just like the beasts."

On that same day he was formed; On that same day he was created; on that same day his form was formed; on that same day a torso was made; on that same day his limbs were attached and his orifices were opened; on that same day breath was given to him. On that same day he stood up on his legs; on that same day he was paired with Eve; on that same day he called all the animals names; on that same day he was brought into the Garden of Eden;

Avot D'Rabbi Natan - Chapter 1

on that same day he was commanded not to eat from the tree; on that same day he disgraced himself; on that same day he was driven out, which fulfills the words of the verse, "Man does not spend even one night in honor."

On that same day they went up into their bed as two and came down as four. Rabbi Yehudah ben Beteira says: On that same day they went up into their bed as two and came down as six. On that same day Adam was given three new decrees, as it says, "And to Adam God said: Because you heeded the voice of your wife………the ground will be cursed because of you. You will eat from it in distres….and it will sprout thorns and thistles for you and you will eat the grasses of the field." When Adam heard that the Holy Blessed One said to him, "You will eat the grasses of the field," immediately his limbs began to shake. He said before God: Master of the World! Will I and my animal eat from the same trough? The Holy Blessed One said: Since your limbs began to shake nizdazu, therefore "by the sweat zeiah of your brow you will be able to eat bread". And just as Adam was given these three decrees, so, too, Eve was given three decrees, as it says, "To the woman God said: I will increase and increase your pangs in childbearing; you will give birth to children in pain." So, when a woman has her menstrual bleeding, the beginning of her cycle is the most difficult for her. "I will increase and increase": When a woman first has sexual relations, at the beginning intercourse is difficult for her. "Your pangs": And when a woman becomes pregnant, her face becomes ugly and greenish for the first three months.

When evening began to descend, Adam looked toward the darkening horizon and said: Woe is me! Because I disgraced myself, the Holy Blessed one is bringing

Avot D'Rabbi Natan - Chapter 1

darkness upon my world. He did not know that this was simply the way of the world. In the morning, when he saw that the world began to brighten from the east, he felt an overwhelming sense of joy. So, he went and built altars, and brought a bull whose horns had grown in before his hooves, and he offered it up as a sacrifice, as it says, "It will be better to the Eternal than a bull with horns and hooves."

The bull that Adam offered up on the altar, as well as the bull that Noah offered up, and the ram that Abraham our forefather offered up in place of his son, all had horns that had grown in before their hooves, as it says, "Abraham raised his eyes, and behold, a ram was caught in the brambles by its horns."

At that same hour, three groups of angels who serve God came down, and in their hands were lyres and harps and all kinds of instruments, and they sang with him, as it says, "A psalm a song for the Sabbath day. It is good to thank the Eternal…and to speak of your kindness in the morning, and your faith through the night." "To speak of your kindness in the morning" – that is the World to Come, which is compared to morning, as it says, "They are renewed in the morning; great is your faith." "And your faith through the night" – that is this world, which is compared to night, as it says, "The burden of Dumah. Someone calls to me from Seir: Watchman, what will happen in the night? Watchman, what will happen in the night?"

At that same hour, the Holy Blessed One said: If I do not punish the snake, I will be found to have caused the destruction of the whole world! They will say, that one, whom I have crowned, and made king over the whole world, how can it be that he has ruined himself and eaten

Avot D'Rabbi Natan - Chapter 1

the fruits of that tree? Immediately, He turned to the snake and cursed it, as it says, "Then the Eternal God said to the snake…." Thus, Rabbi Yosei said: If this verse had not concluded with its curse, the whole world would have been destroyed.

When the Holy Blessed One created the first human being, He formed it facing both frontward and backward, as it says, "You formed me after and before, and you placed your hand upon me." And the angels who serve God came down to serve Him in order to destroy the first human being. So, the Holy Blessed One took it and placed it under His wings, as it says, "You hedge me before and behind, and you placed your hands upon me."

Another interpretation of "And you placed your hands upon me": When Adam disgraced himself, the Holy Blessed One took one of His hands away. From here we see that both the human being and the Sanctuary, when they were created, were created by God's two hands. From where do we learn that the human being was created with God's two hands? As it says, "Your hands made me and fashioned me." From where do we learn that the Sanctuary was created with God's two hands? As it says, "In the Sanctuary, God, which your hands have established." It also states, "He brought them to the border of His Sanctuary, the mountain which His right hand had acquired."

And it says, "The Eternal will reign forever and ever."

Avot D'Rabbi Natan - Chapter 2

Chapter 2

What is the fence that the Torah made around its words? It says, "Do not come near woman during her period of impurity." Perhaps you would still think one could hug her and kiss her and speak flirtatiously with her. So, the verse tells you, "Do not come near." Perhaps you would still think one could sleep next to her on the bed, as long as she was clothed. So, the verse tells you, "Do not come near." Perhaps you would still think she could wash her face and put makeup on her eyes. So, the verse tells you, "She is in her period of exile" – that is, all the days that she is in her period of impurity, she will be in exile. Because of this they said: The spirit of the sages is pleased with anyone who makes herself unattractive during the days of her period of impurity. The spirit of the sages is displeased with anyone who makes herself attractive during the days of her period of impurity.

There is a story of a man who studied much Scripture and much Mishnah, and devotedly served the great Torah scholars – and yet he died in middle age. So, his wife took his tefillin and went to the synagogues and study houses, and would scream and cry and say to them: My masters! It is written in your Torah, "For it is your life, and the length of your days." But my husband studied so much Scripture, and so much Mishnah, and served the Torah scholars so devotedly – so why did he die in middle age? No one there had anything to say in response. Then one day, Elijah the prophet visited her and said: My daughter, why are you screaming and crying? She said to him: Master, my husband studied so much Scripture, and so much Mishnah, and devotedly served the Torah scholars – and yet he died in middle age. He said to her: When you

Avot D'Rabbi Natan - Chapter 2

were in your period of impurity, did he come near you during the first three days? She said to him, "God forbid! He never touched me with even his little finger. And he would say to me, do not even touch the dishes, lest they bring me to doubt whether or not I am impure. Elijah continued: And during the latter days, did he come near you? She said to him: Master, I ate with and drank with him, and slept with him in the same bed fully clothed, and yes, his flesh would touch my flesh – but we never had any intention of doing anything else. He said to her: Blessed is the Omnipresent God who killed him! For so it is written in the Torah, "Do not come near a woman during her period of impurity."

It says, "None of you shall come near any of his own flesh." Because of this, they said: A man should not be alone with any women in an inn, even with his sister or his daughter, because of what people will think. He should not chat with a woman in the marketplace, even with his own wife, let alone with another woman, because of what people will claim. A man should not follow a woman in the marketplace, not even his own wife, let alone another woman, because of what people will claim. It says here, "None of you shall come near," and then it says further on in the verse, "Do not come near." Do not come near something that causes you to sin. Stay away from ugliness, and even something similar to ugliness. Therefore, the sages said: Stay away from a minor sin, for it may bring you to a major sin. And run to perform a minor mitzvah commandment, for it will bring you to perform a major mitzvah.

It says, "Your belly is like a heap of wheat, surrounded by a hedge of lilies." "Your belly is like a heap of wheat" – that refers to the congregation of Israel. "Surrounded by

Avot D'Rabbi Natan - Chapter 2

a hedge of lilies" – that refers to the seventy elders.

Another interpretation: "Your belly is a heap of wheat" – these are the minor, easy commandments. "Surrounded by a hedge of lilies" – when Israel performs mitzvot commandments, they are taken into the life of the World to Come. How does this happen? When one's wife is in her period of impurity, and she is with him in his house, he wants to sleep with her – he wants to, but he does not. Will anyone see him, or will anyone know, or say anything to him? He is only afraid of the one who checks the immersion at the mikveh. You could say the same about taking challa for the priests, and you could say that same about giving the first shearing of wool to the priests. These are minor, easy commandments – like lilies – but when Israel performs them, they are taken into the life of the World to Come.

What is the fence that Moses made around his words? It says, "The Eternal said to Moses: Go to the people, and keep them holy, today and tomorrow." But Moses the Righteous did not want to say this to them the way that the Holy Blessed One said it to him. So instead, he said this to them: "Prepare yourselves: for three days do not go near a woman." Moses added an extra day for them on his own. For this is what Moses reasoned to himself: A man will go be with his wife on the first day and then his semen will come out of her on the third day, and then they will be ritually impure. And so, Israel will receive words of Torah from Mount Sinai while in a state of impurity! Instead, I will add a third day for them so that no man goes to be with his wife, and no semen will come out of her on the third day, and they will be ritually pure and so they will receive Torah from Mount Sinai in a state of purity.

Avot D'Rabbi Natan - Chapter 2

This is one of the things that Moses decided on his own as a more strict ruling, and his decision was in accordance with the will of the Omnipresent God. He broke the tablets, and his decision was in accordance with the will of the Omnipresent God. He stayed outside the Tent of Meeting, and his decision was in accordance with the will of the Omnipresent God. He stayed apart from his wife, and his decision was in accordance with the will of the Omnipresent God. How so? He said to himself: If Israel need only remain in a state of holiness for a short period of time, and need only be ready to receive the Ten Commandments from Mount Sinai, and yet the Holy Blessed One said to me, "Go to the people, and keep them holy, today and tomorrow"; then I, who am appointed to receive the Divine Countenance every day, at every moment, and do not know when He will speak with me, nor whether it will be during the day or at night – all the more so must I stay apart from my wife! And his decision was in accordance with the will of the Omnipresent God. Rabbi Yehudah ben Beteira said: He did not stay apart from his wife until he was told to straight from mouth of the Almighty, as it says, "Mouth to mouth I speak to him"; that is, mouth to mouth I told him to stay apart from his wife, and so he did. Another opinion also held that Moses did not stay apart from his wife until he was told to straight from the mouth of the Almighty, but derived it instead from these verses: "Go and tell them to return to their tents," and then after that it says, "But you stay here with Me." So Moses returned to God and stayed apart from his wife, and his decision was in accordance with the will of the Omnipresent God.

He stayed outside the Tent of Meeting. How so? He said to himself: If my brother Aaron, who was anointed with

Avot D'Rabbi Natan - Chapter 2

the anointing oil, and wrapped in the priestly garments, and is able to use all these things in a state of holiness, and yet the Holy Blessed One said to me, "Tell your brother Aaron he may not come any time he wishes into the Sanctuary"; then I, who am never allowed in – all the more so should I stay outside the Tent of Meeting! So, he stayed outside the Tent of Meeting, and his decision was in accordance with the will of the Omnipresent God.

He broke the tablets. How so? They say that when Moses went up on High to receive the tablets, he found that they had already been written and set aside during the six days of Creation, as it says, "And the tablets were the work of God, and the writing was God's writing, engraved there upon the tablets." Do not read "engraved" harut, but "freedom" herut, for anyone who labors in Torah makes himself a free man. At that moment, the angels who serve God pinned an accusation on Moses, saying: Master of the World, it says, "What is the human that you should be mindful of him, the son of man that you should take note of him? You have made him a little less than God, and crowned him with glory and splendor. You have set him up to rule over your handiwork. The world is beneath your feet. Sheep, oxen, and all of them, and wild beasts as well. The birds of the heavens and the fish of the sea." So, they spoke behind Moses' back and asked: Why is this one, born of an earthly woman, worthy of ascending to the heights? As it says, "You went up to the heights, having taken captives, having taken gifts." He took them and went down, and was overjoyed. But when he saw that they were disgracing themselves with the Golden Calf, he said to himself: How can I give them these tablets? I will be binding them in serious commandments, and causing them to deserve death from Above! For it is written on

Avot D'Rabbi Natan - Chapter 2

these tablets, "You shall have no other gods before me". So he started to go back up. The seventy elders saw him and ran after him. He was holding on to one end of the tablets, and they grabbed on to the other end. But Moses' strength was greater than all of theirs, as it says, "And for all the awesome power that Moses displayed before all of Israel." He looked and saw that the writing was flying off them, and he said: How can I give these tablets to Israel? For there is nothing on them! So instead, I will take a hold of them and smash them, as it says, "I grabbed the two tablets, and I cast them out of my two hands, and I broke them." Rabbi Yosei HaGalili says: I will give you a parable. To what can this be compared? It can be compared to a human king who said to his messenger: Go out and betroth to me a beautiful, gracious maiden, whose deeds are lovely. The messenger went and betrothed such a woman. But after he betrothed her, he went and found her cheating with someone else. He made an instant a fortiori judgment with himself and said: If I give her the marriage contract now, she will immediately deserve death. So, let her instead be released from my master forever. So, too, did Moses the Righteous make an a fortiori judgment with himself, and said: How can I give these tablets to Israel and bind them in serious commandments and cause them to deserve death? For it is written upon them. "One who sacrifices to any gods other than the Eternal alone will be put to death." So instead I will take a hold of them and smash them, and thereby return the people to good standing, lest Israel say: Where are the first tablets that you brought down? These things are counterfeit! Rabbi Yehudah ben Beteira says: Moses did not break the tablets until he was told to straight from the mouth of the Almighty, as it says,

Avot D'Rabbi Natan - Chapter 2

"Mouth to mouth I speak to him" – that is, mouth to mouth I said to him: Break the tablets! And there are others who say: Moses did not break the tablets until he was told to straight from the mouth of the Almighty, as it says, "I saw there that you had sinned against the Eternal your God." It says only, "I saw there," because he saw the writing flying off the tablets. Others say: Moses did not break the tablets until he was told to straight from the mouth of the Almighty, as it says, "The tablets were there, as the Eternal had commanded me." It says only, "commanded me," because first he was commanded to break them, and then he broke them. Rabbi Elazar ben Azariah says: Moses did not break the tablets until he was told to straight from the mouth of the Almighty, as it says, "...that Moses performed before all of Israel." Just as later on he was commanded and then did, so too here, he was commanded and then did. Rabbi Akiva says: Moses did not break the tablets until he was told to straight from the mouth of the Almighty, as it said, "I took a hold of the two tablets." A person can take a hold only of that which he has been permitted by his Creator. Rabbi Meir says: Moses did not break the tablets until he was told to straight from the mouth of the Almighty, as it says, "That asher which you broke": Well done yishar koach that you broke them!

King Hezekiah decided four things, and his decision was in accordance with the will of the Omnipresent God. He hid the Book of Healing, and his decision was in accordance with the will of the Omnipresent God. He broke apart the copper snake, and his decision was in accordance with the will of the Omnipresent God, "Until those days, the children of Israel had been burning incense to it, and it was called Nekhushatan the snake

Avot D'Rabbi Natan - Chapter 2

god". He removed the shrines and altars, and his decision was in accordance with the will of the Omnipresent God, as it says, "Hezekiah removed His shrines and His altars and spoke to Judah and Jerusalem, and said: Will you bow down before one altar, and burn incense upon it?" He stopped up the waters of Gihon, and his decision was in accordance with the will of the Omnipresent God, as it says, "Hezekiah stopped up the spring of the waters of upper Gihon, leading it downward, west of the City of David. And Hezekiah was successful in all that he did."

What was the fence that Job made around his words? It says, "A pure and righteous man, who fears God and turns away from evil." This teaches us that Job distanced himself from anything that would bring him to sin, from any ugliness, and from anything even resembling ugliness. If that is so, then why do we have to also learn that he was "a pure and righteous man"? But instead, this is here to teach us that Job emerged from the womb already circumcised. Adam also emerged already circumcised, as it says, "And God created the person in His image." Seth also emerged already circumcised, as it says, "He had a child in his likeness and image." Noah also emerged already circumcised, as it says, "A just and pure man in his generation." Shem also emerged already circumcised, as it says, "Malkitzedek, king of Shalem." Jacob also emerged already circumcised, as it says, "Jacob was a pure man, who sat in tents." Joseph also emerged already circumcised, as it says, "This is the progeny of Jacob: Joseph." But shouldn't it say instead: This is the progeny of Jacob: Reuben? What do we learn from the fact that it says Joseph? We learn that just as Jacob emerged already circumcised, so, too Joseph emerged already circumcised. Moses also emerged

Avot D'Rabbi Natan - Chapter 2

already circumcised, as it says, "She saw that he was good." And what did his mother see in him that was lovelier and more praiseworthy than any other person? That he emerged circumcised. Bil'am the wicked also came out circumcised, as it says, "The word of him who hears God's speech." Samuel also emerged circumcised, as it says – "Young Samuel continued to grow and was good." David also emerged circumcised – as it says, "A mikhtam of David. Protect me, for I seek refuge in you." Jeremiah also emerged already circumcised, as it says, "Before I formed you in the belly, I knew you; and before you came out of the womb, I consecrated you." Zerubbabel also emerged already circumcised, as it says, "On that day I will take, declares the Eternal of Hosts, I will take Zerubbabel son of Shealtiel, declares the Eternal." And it says, "I have made a covenant with my eyes, so how can I gaze at a maiden [i.e., an unmarried woman]?" This teaches that Job was strict with himself and would not even look at a maiden. And if with a maiden – whom he could marry if he wished to his son, to his daughter, or to another family member – he was strict with himself and would not look at her, then all the more so would he never look at a married woman! And why was he so strict with himself not to look even at a maiden? Because Job said to himself: Perhaps I will look today, and tomorrow another man will come along and marry her, and then I will have looked at a married woman.

What is the fence that the Prophets made around their words? It says, "The Eternal goes forth like a warrior, like a man of war He rouses His rage. He yells, He roars aloud." Not like one warrior, but like all the warriors in the world. Similarly, "A lion has roared; who will not

Avot D'Rabbi Natan - Chapter 2

fear? My Lord God has spoken; who will not prophesy?" Not like one lion, but like all the lions in the world. Similarly, "And there, the Presence of the God of Israel, coming from the east with a roar like the roar of the mighty waters; and the earth was lit up by His Presence." "Like the roar of the mighty waters" – this is the angel Gabriel. "And the earth was lit up by His Presence" – this is the face of the **Shekhinah** is the Divine Presence of God. And is it not all the more so that if Gabriel, who was but one of many thousands and thousands, and tens and tens of thousands, who stand before God, had a roar that went from one end of the world to the other, then the King of all kings, the Holy Blessed One, who created the whole world, created the upper realms and created the lower realms, even more so! But they show the eye only what it can see and let the ear hear only what it can hear.

What is the fence that the Writings made around their words? It says, "Keep your path far away from her, and do not go near the doorway of her house." "Keep your path far away from her" – that is heresy. For they tell people: Do not go among heretics. Do not enter there, lest you they cause you to stumble. And what if someone says: I trust myself, and even though I go there, they will not cause me to stumble. For maybe you will say: I will listen to what they have to say, but I will come back. But the verse teaches us, "All who go to her cannot return and find again the paths of life."

It is written, "She has prepared the feast, mixed the wine, and also set the table." These are the wicked who, when a person comes in and sits among them, feed him and give him drink, and dress him and cover him, and give him lots of money. But when he has become one of them, each one picks out what belongs to them, and takes it back from

Avot D'Rabbi Natan - Chapter 2

him. About them it says, "He follows her until the arrow pierces his liver. He is like a bird rushing into a trap, unknowingly."

Another interpretation of "Keep your path far away from her": This is a prostitute. For they tell people: Do not go to that marketplace, and do not enter into that alleyway, for there is a beautiful and celebrated prostitute there. But he says: I trust myself, and even though I go there, she will not cause me to stumble. They say to him: Even though you trust yourself, do not go there, for maybe she will cause you to stumble. For the sages said that a person should not accustom himself to passing by the door of a prostitute. As it says, "For many are those she has struck dead, and numerous are her victims."

What is the fence that the sages made around their words? The sages said: the Shema of the evening prayer may be recited until midnight Rabban Gamliel said: Until the rooster crows. When a person comes home from work, he should not say: I'll eat a little, and drink a little, and sleep a little, and then afterward, I'll recite the Shema. He may end up sleeping the whole night and not reciting. Rather, a person coming home from work in the evening should go straight to the house of prayer or to the house of study. If he is accustomed to read Scripture, he should study that first; if he is accustomed to recite Mishnah, he should study that first. If not, he should recite the Shema, and then finish praying. Anyone who violates the words of the sages deserves death. Rabban Gamliel said: Sometimes a person recites it twice – once at night, before the dawn has broken, and once after the dawn has broken. Then he will have fulfilled his obligation both for the day and for the night. Thus, the sages arose and added extra strictures, and made a fence for their words.

Avot D'Rabbi Natan - Chapter 2

And raise up many students. For the House of Shammai, say: One should teach only a person who is wise, humble, of good pedigree, and rich. But the House of Hillel say: Teach everyone, for there were many sinners in Israel, and they were brought close to Torah study, and they came out righteous, kind, and proper.

Avot D'Rabbi Natan - Chapter 3

Chapter 3

Rabbi Akiva says: Anyone who takes a perutah from charity when he does not need to will not die before he comes to need help from others. He would also say: One who wraps rags around his eyes and around his thighs, and says, Give to this blind man, to this boil-infected man! – In the end his words will come true. He would also say: One who casts bread to the ground, or throws money around in anger, will not die before he comes to need help from others.

He would also say: One who tears his clothes in anger, or breaks dishes in anger, in the end he will worship idols. For that is the craftiness of the evil urge: today it says to him, tear your clothes! And then tomorrow it says to him, Worship idols!

He would also say: Someone who looks at his wife and wishes that she will die so that he can inherit from her, or that she will die so that he can marry her sister, or someone who looks at his brother and wishes that he will die so that he can marry his brother's wife, in the end he will be buried during their lifetimes. About such a person Scripture says, "One who digs a pit will fall into it; one who breaks through a fence will be bitten by a snake."

There is a story of a man who ignored the words of Rabbi Akiva and pulled off a woman's head covering in public. She came before Rabbi Akiva and he obligated the man to give her 400 zuz. He replied: Rabbi, give me time. He gave him time. Then what happened? His friend said to him: I will give you some advice. Don't give her even one perutah. Then the friend said: Go take an issar's-worth of oil, and smash the jar on the woman's doorstep. What did the woman do? She went out of her house and uncovered

Avot D'Rabbi Natan - Chapter 3

her head in public and started collecting oil and rubbing it on her head with her hand. He had witnesses who saw her, so he came before Rabbi Akiva and said to him: I have to give this shameful woman 400 zuz? For an issar's-worth of oil, she is willing to dishonor herself. She came out of her house and uncovered her hair in public and was collecting oil and rubbing it on her head with her hand! Rabbi Akiva said to him: What you're saying is meaningless, for although one is not allowed to do harm to himself, one is nevertheless free from punishment. But if others do harm to him, they deserve punishment. So she, who harmed herself, is free from punishment. But you, who harmed her – go and give her 400 zuz.

Rabbi Dostai son of Rabbi Yannai says: If you decided to plant in the first quarter, go back and plant in the second quarter, for perhaps hail will come down upon the world, and the earlier ones will be destroyed while the later ones will survive. For you do not know which will succeed, this one or that one, or if both will survive and they both are equally good or if both are equally bad; as it says, "Sow your seed in the morning, and do not hold back your hand in the evening." If you decided to plant in the first and second quarters, go back and plant in the third quarter, for perhaps a disease will come to the world, and the earlier ones will become diseased while the later ones survive. "For you do not know which will succeed, this one or that one, or if both are equally good," as it says, "Sow your seed in the morning."

Rabbi Yishmael son of Rabbi Yosei says: Study Torah in your old age. If you studied Torah in your youth, do not say: I don't have to study in my old age. Rather, study Torah, for you do not know which period of study will be most beneficial. If you studied Torah at a time of wealth,

Avot D'Rabbi Natan - Chapter 3

do not turn away from it at time of poverty. If you studied Torah at a time of satiation, do not turn away from it at a time of hunger. If you studied Torah at a time of leisure, do not turn away from it at a time of stress. For it is better for a person to have one thing during a crisis than a hundred in the midst of abundance as it says, "For you do not know if they will both be equally good", as it says, "Sow your seed in the morning, and do not hold back your hand in the evening."

Rabbi Akiva says: If you studied Torah in your youth study Torah in your old age, do not say: I don't have to study in my old age; for you do not know which will be the most beneficial, if both will stay with you, or if both will be equally good, as it says, "Sow your seed in the morning."

Rabbi Meir says: If you studied with one teacher, do not say: That's enough for me. Rather, go to another sage and study Torah. But do not go to just anyone. Rather, go to someone who has been close to you from the start, as it says, "Drink water from your own cistern, that which flows from your own well."

Every person has an obligation to apprentice with three Torah scholars, such as Rabbi Eliezer, Rabbi Yehoshua, and Rabbi Akiva, as it says, "Happy is the person who hears me come early to my doors every day, and waits outside my opening." Do not read it as "doors," but "a door and two doors" a total of three, for you do not know if two of them will work for you, or if two of them will be equally good, as it says, "Sow your seed in the morning."

Rabbi Yehoshua says: Marry a woman in your youth, and marry a woman in your old age. Have children in your youth, and have children in your old age. Do not say: I

Avot D'Rabbi Natan - Chapter 3

will not marry a woman. Rather, marry a woman and have sons and daughters, and be fruitful and multiply greatly in the world. For you do not know if both of them will work out for you, or if both of them will be equally good, as it says, "Sow your seed in the morning."

He would also say: If you give a perutah to a poor person in the morning, and then another poor person is standing before you in the evening, give to him as well. For you do not know if both of them will be sustained through you, or if both of them are equally good, as it says, "Sow your seed in the morning."

There is a story of a certain righteous man who gave one dinar to a poor person during a time of famine. His wife derided him. So, he went and slept in the graveyard on the eve of Rosh Hashanah and heard two spirits of dead girls talking to one another. The first one said to the other: My friend, come and fly across the world with me and we will see what disasters are coming upon the world. The second one said: My friend, I cannot go, because I am trapped under a thicket of reeds. So, you go, and tell me what you hear. She went and came back, and her friend said: My friend, did you hear anything behind the curtain about what disasters are coming upon the world? She said: I heard that hail will strike anyone who plants in the first quarter. So righteous man went and planted in the second quarter. Hail struck everyone else, but did not strike him. The next year, he went and slept again in the graveyard, and he heard the two spirits talking to one another. The first one said to the other: Come, let us fly across the world and we will see what disasters are coming upon the world. The second one said: My friend, didn't I say to you I cannot go, because I am trapped under a thicket of reeds. So, you go, and tell me what you

Avot D'Rabbi Natan - Chapter 3

hear. She went and came back, and her friend said: My friend, did you hear anything behind the curtain about what disasters are coming upon the world? She replied: I heard that crop disease will strike anyone who plants in the second quarter. So righteous man went and planted in the first quarter. Crop disease came upon the world. Everyone else's crops became diseased, but his did not become diseased. He told his wife the whole story. One day, the saint's wife got into an argument with the mother of one of the dead girls. The righteous man's wife said to the mother: Come, I will show you your daughter, trapped under a thicket of reeds. The next year, the righteous man went and slept in the graveyard, and he heard the two spirits talking to one another. The first one said: My friend, come and fly across the world with me, and we will hear what they are saying behind the curtain. The second one replied to her: My friend, leave me be. Things that were spoken between us have been overheard by the living.

There is a story of a certain saint who would regularly give charity. Once he went and sat on a boat, and a wind came along, and his boat sank into the sea. Rabbi Akiva saw it happen, and came before the court to testify that his wife was free to marry again. Before he had a chance to get up, that very man came in and stood before him. Rabbi Akiva said: Are you the one who sank in the sea? He replied: Yes. Rabbi Akiva continued: And who brought you up out of the sea? He replied: The charity I gave is what brought me up out of the sea. Rabbi Akiva said: How do you know that? He replied: When I went down into the depths of the abyss, I heard a voice coming from the roar of the waves, each one saying to the other, Come, let us crash together and raise this man up from

Avot D'Rabbi Natan - Chapter 3

the sea, for he gave charity all of his life. Immediately, Rabbi Akiva opened his mouth and said: Blessed is God, the God of Israel, who chose the words of the Torah and the words of the sages, for the words of the Torah and the words of the sages endure forever and ever! For it says, "Send your bread forth upon the waters, for after many days, you will find it," and it also says, "And charity saves from death."

There is a story of Benjamin the Righteous, who was in charge of the charity box. A woman came before him and said to him: Master, provide for me! He said to her: The fact is, there is nothing at all in the charity box. She said to him: Master, if you do not provide for me, I will surely die, along with my four children. So he provided for her from his own funds. After some time, Benjamin the Righteous became ill, and was in lying in bed in pain. The angels who serve God said before the Holy Blessed One" Master of the World! You said that anyone who sustains even one soul in Israel Scripture regards them as if they had sustained the whole world. And Benjamin the Righteous, who sustained a widow and her four children – all the more so! But there he lies in his bed in illness and pain. Immediately, they begged for mercy for him, they ripped up the scroll of his judgment, and they added twenty-two years to his life.

Avot D'Rabbi Natan - Chapter 4

Chapter 4

Shimon the Righteous was one of the last surviving members of the Men of the Great Assembly. He would say: The world stands on three things: on the Torah, on the Temple service, and on acts of kindness.

On the Torah; How so? It says, "I desire kindness, not a well-being offering zevach, and the knowledge of God, which comes from studying Torah more than burnt offerings olot." From here we learn that the burnt offering is more beloved than the well-being offering, because the burnt offering is entirely consumed in the fires, as it says, "The priest shall turn the whole thing into smoke on the altar." And in another place, it says, "Samuel took one milking lamb, and offered it to be consumed, as a burnt offering to the Eternal." And the study of Torah is more beloved before the Omnipresent God than offerings, for if a person studies Torah, he comes to have knowledge of the Omnipresent God, as it says, "Then you will understand the awe of the Eternal and you will discover the knowledge of God." From here we learn that when a sage sit and expounds before the congregation, Scripture considers it as if he brought fat and blood upon the altar.

If two Torah scholars are sitting and laboring in the Torah, and a bridal or funeral procession passes by, if there are already enough people participating, these two should not leave their studying; but if not, they should get up and offer words of Torah and praise to the bride, or escort the dead.

There is a story of Rabbi Yehudah son of Rabbi Elai, who was sitting and teaching his students, and bride passed by and grabbed him by the hand, because they needed him, and so he offered her words of Torah until she passed by.

Avot D'Rabbi Natan - Chapter 4

There was another story of Rabbi Yehudah son of Rabbi Elai, who was sitting and teaching his students, and a bride passed by and he said: What is this? And they said to him: A bride is passing. He said to them: My children stand and attend to the bride, for thus we find that the Holy Blessed One attended to a bride as it says, "The Eternal God built the rib". If God attended to a bride – then I, all the more so! And where do we find that the Holy Blessed One attended to a bride? As it says, "The Eternal God built the rib" – and this is what they call braiding in seaside towns: "building." From here we learn that the Holy Blessed One Prepared Eve and made her up as a bride and brought her before Adam, as it says, "And He brought her to Adam." Once upon a time, the Holy Blessed One acted as a companion to Adam; from that point forward, Adam had acquired a companion of his own as it says, "Bone of my bone, flesh of my flesh". Eve was taken from the rib of Adam once; from that point forward, a person marries his fellow's daughter.

On the Temple service; How so? While the Holy Temple was still standing, the land was blessed for its inhabitants and rains fell at the proper time, as it says, "To love the Eternal your God and to serve Him with all your heart and all your soul, and I will give you rain in your land in season, the early rain and the late…and I will give grass to your fields for your animals." And when the Temple is not standing, the land is not blessed for its inhabitants and the rains do not come in season, as it says, "Guard yourselves from your heart's temptation…and He will shut up the heavens and there will be no rain." And so it says, "Take note, from this day and beforehand, before any stone had been placed on a stone in the House of the Eternal, if one came to a heap of wheat of twenty

Avot D'Rabbi Natan - Chapter 4

measures, it would yield only ten; and if one came to the wine barrel to skim off fifty measures, the press would yield only twenty." Why doesn't it say also for the wine barrel, twenty and then ten, just as it does for the wheat, twenty and then ten? As the wine barrel is a more exalted symbol than the wheat. This teaches you that when the wine is cursed, there is a bad sign upon the whole year. Israel said before the Holy Blessed One: Master of the World! Why do you do this to us? A holy spirit answered them, "You came for a lot, but there is only a little…because My House is destroyed, but you all run to your own houses." And if you would perform the Temple services, I would bless you as I once did, as it says, "Take note…from the twenty-fourth day of the ninth month, from the day the foundation was laid for the House of the Eternal…is the seed yet in the granary? And have the grape, and the fig, and the pomegranate, and the olive tree yet borne fruit? From that day I will send blessing." This teaches you that there is no service dearer to the Holy Blessed One than the service of the Holy Temple.

On acts of kindness; How so? It says, "For I desire kindness, not a well-being offering." The world was created from the very beginning with kindness, as it says, "For I have said that the world will be built on kindness, and the heavens will be established on your faith." Once, Rabban our rabbi Yohanan ben Zakkai, left Jerusalem, and Rabbi Yehoshua followed after him. And he saw the Holy Temple destroyed. Rabbi Yehoshua said: Woe to us, for this is destroyed – the place where all of Israel's sins are forgiven! Rabbi Yohanan said to him: My son, do not be distressed, for we have a form of atonement just like it. And what is it? Acts of kindness, as it says, "For I desire kindness, not a well-being offering." And so, we

Avot D'Rabbi Natan - Chapter 4

find that Daniel, the precious man, would busy himself with acts of kindness. And what were these acts of kindness that he was so busy with? If you would say that in fact, he did bring burnt offerings and other sacrifices in Babylon, doesn't it already say, "Take care not to bring burnt offerings in just any place you see, but only in the place that the Eternal will choose in one of your tribal territories shall you bring burnt offerings." So, what were the acts of kindness he busied himself with? He would help a bride and bring her happiness, he would escort the dead in a funeral procession, and he would always give a perutah to a poor person. And he would pray three times a day, and his prayers would be gladly accepted, as it says, "When Daniel learned that the ban against worshiping God had been put in writing, he went to his house, in whose upper chamber he had windows made facing Jerusalem, and three times a day he knelt down, prayed, and made a confession to his God, as he had always done."

And when Vespasian came to destroy Jerusalem, he said to the inhabitants: Fools! Why do you seek to destroy this city and burn the Holy Temple? What do I request of you? Only that you give me one bow or one arrow as a sign of your surrender, and then I will leave you be. They said to him: Just as we went out to battle against the two who came before you, and killed them, so will we go out against you and kill you. When Rabban Yohanan ben Zakkai heard this, he sent for the men of Jerusalem and said to them: My children, why do seek to destroy this city and burn the Holy Temple? For what did he ask of you but one bow or one arrow, and then he would leave you be. They said to him: Just as we went out to battle against the two who came before him, and we killed them,

Avot D'Rabbi Natan - Chapter 4

so will we go out against him and kill him. Vespasian had men lurking within the walls of Jerusalem, and everything they heard they would write on an arrow and shoot over the wall. So, they reported that Rabban Yohanan ben Zakkai supported the Caesar. Thus, would he remind the men of Jerusalem, and plead with them to acquiesce to Vespasian. And after Rabban Yohanan ben Zakkai said this to them day after day, and saw that they would not accept his advice, he sent for his students, Rabbi Eliezer and Rabbi Yehoshua, and said to them: My sons take me out of this place! Make me a coffin, and I will sleep in it. So, Rabbi Eliezer held the coffin on one end, and Rabbi Yehoshua held it on the other, and they carried him until the sun set, right up to the gates of Jerusalem. The gatekeepers said to them: What is this? They replied: A dead body – and you know that a corpse cannot remain overnight in Jerusalem. They said: If that is a dead body, go ahead and take it out of the city. So, they took him out, and were carrying him until sunset until they came to Vespasian, and they opened the coffin, and Rabbi Yohanan got up and stood before him. He said: So, you are Rabbi Yohanan ben Zakkai. Ask for whatever you wish, and I will give it to you. He replied: I ask nothing from you except for Yavneh. I will go there and teach my students, and I will establish prayer, and I will do all the mitzvot mentioned in the Torah. Vespasian replied: Go. All that you wish to do, you may do. Rabbi Yohanan said to him: Do you want me to tell you one thing? He said: Go ahead. He said to him: Take note; soon you will ascend to the kingship. How do you know? Vespasian said to him. Rabbi Yohanan answered: We have a tradition that the Holy Temple will not be taken by an ordinary man, but only by a king. For it says, "And the

Avot D'Rabbi Natan - Chapter 4

Lebanon tree will fall in its majesty." They say that it was not one or two or three days until a letter came from Vespasian's city announcing that the Caesar had died and they were appointing him to ascend to the kingship. They brought him a catapult and positioned it toward the walls of Jerusalem. Then they brought him cedar posts, put them in the catapult, and fired them against the wall until they made a breach. Then they brought him the head of a pig, put it in the catapult, and flung it toward the sacrificial portions that were on the Temple altar.

While Jerusalem was being taken, Rabban Yohanan ben Zakkai was sitting and waiting, and he trembled before God, just as Eli sat and watched, as it says, "There was Eli, sitting on a seat on the side of the road, waiting, and his heart trembled because of the Ark of God." When Rabban Yohanan ben Zakkai heard that Jerusalem was destroyed and the Holy Temple was burning in flames, he tore his clothes, and his students tore their clothes, and they cried and screamed and lamented.

It says, "Open your doors, Lebanon the Holy Temple, and let fire consume your cedars" – these are the high priests who were in the Sanctuary, who took their keys in their hands and threw them toward the heavens, and said before the Holy Blessed One: Master of the World! Here are your keys, which you entrusted to us. For we were not faithful custodians doing the King's work and eating from the King's table.

Abraham, Isaac, and Jacob, and the twelve tribes, were also crying and screaming and lamenting, and they said, "Howl, cypresses, for cedars have fallen! How the mighty are ravaged!" "How, cypresses, for cedars have fallen!" – these are Abraham, Isaac, and Jacob, and the twelve tribes. "Howl, you oaks of Bashan" – these are Moses,

Avot D'Rabbi Natan - Chapter 4

Aaron, and Miriam. "For the stately forest is laid low" – that is the Holy of Holies. The voice of wailing shepherds, for their fields have been ravaged these are David and his son Solomon. "The sound of the lions roaring, for the jungle of the Jordan has been ravaged" – these are Elijah and Elisha.

The Holy Blessed One makes people different from one another in three ways: in voice, in disposition, and in appearance. Why did the Holy Blessed One make one person different from another in voice? Had He not made different voices, there would be more illicit sexual relations in the world. When a man left his house, another would come along and subdue his wife in his own house. Therefore, the Holy Blessed One variated the sounds of voices, so that no one voice sounded like any other. Why disposition? The Holy Blessed one made one person's disposition different from another's, for if the Holy Blessed One had not made every person with a different disposition, then everyone would be jealous of one another. Therefore, the Holy Blessed One variated disposition, so that no one person's disposition was like any others. Why different appearance? The Holy Blessed One made one person's appearance different from another's, for if the Holy Blessed One had not made one person's appearance look different from another's, then the women of Israel would not recognize their husbands, and the men would not recognize their wives. Therefore, the Holy Blessed One made every person with a different face.

Avot D'Rabbi Natan - Chapter 5

Chapter 5

Antigonus, a man of Sokho, received from Shimon the Righteous. He would say: Do not be like servants who attend upon their master only on the condition that they receive a reward. Rather, be like servants who attend upon their master only on the condition that they do not receive a reward. And let the awe of the heavens be upon you so that your compensation will be double in the future.

Antigonus, a man of Sokho, had two students who were studying his words. They would then teach them to other students, who would then teach them to yet other students. Those students then questioned what they had learned and said: Why did our fathers say such a thing? Is it possible that a worker should labor all day and not receive his compensation in the evening? If our fathers had known that there was another world, and that the dead would be revived, they would not have said this. So, they decided to separate from the way of the Torah. Two factions emerged from them: the Sadducees and the Baitusees. The Sadducees Tzadukim were called that because of Tzadok, and the Baitusees because of Baitus. And they would make a point of always using gold and silver things, not because they were so enamoured of them, but because they said: The Pharisees have a tradition that they will deny themselves in this world. Yet in the next world they will have nothing!

Avot D'Rabbi Natan - Chapter 6

Chapter 6

Yosei ben Yoezer said: Let your house be a gathering place for the sages.

How so? This teaches us that a person's house should always be open to the sages, and to their students, and their students' students, so that a person should be able to say to his friend: I will save a place for you there! Another explanation: How should your house be a gathering place for the sages? When a student of the sages enters and says: Teach me! – If you have something to teach, teach it, but if not, let him go on his way. He should not sit before you on a bed, or a chair, or a bench. He should sit before you only on the ground. And anything that comes out of your mouth, he should accept with reverence, fear, quaking, and trembling.

Become dirty in the dust of their feet. How so? When a Torah scholar enters the city, do not say: I don't need him. Instead, go to him. And do not sit next to him on a bed, or on a chair, or on a bench. Rather, sit before him on the ground, and accept upon yourself every word that comes from his mouth with fear and reverence, trembling and sweating, just as our forefathers accepted what they heard at Mount Sinai with fear and reverence, trembling and sweating.

Another explanation: Become dirty in the dust of their feet: This refers to Rabbi Eliezer; and drink in their words thirstily: This refers to Rabbi Akiva.

What were the origins of Rabbi Akiva? They say that he was forty years old and had still not learned anything. Once, he was standing at the mouth of a well and he said: Who carved a hole in this stone? They said to him: It is from the water, which constantly falls on it, day after day.

Avot D'Rabbi Natan - Chapter 6

And they said: Akiva, don't you know this from the verse, "Water erodes stones"? Rabbi Akiva immediately applied this, all the more so, to himself. He said: If something soft can carve something hard, then all the more so, the words of Torah, which are like steel, can engrave themselves on my heart, which is but flesh and blood. He immediately went to start studying Torah. He went with his son and they sat down by the schoolteachers. He said to one: Rabbi, teach me Torah! He then took hold of one end of the tablet, and his son took hold of the other end. The teacher wrote down aleph and beit for him, and he learned them aleph to tav, and he learned them; the book of Leviticus, and he learned it. And he went on studying until he learned the whole Torah. Then he went and sat before Rabbi Eliezer and Rabbi Joshua. My masters, he said, open up the sense of the Mishnah to me. When they told him one law, he went off and sat down to work it out for himself. This aleph – what was it written for? That beit – what was it written for? Why was this thing said? He kept coming back, and kept asking them, until he reduced his teachers to silence. Rabbi Shimon ben Elazar said: I will give you a parable to tell you what this was like: Like a stonecutter who was hacking away at the mountains. One time he took his pickaxe in his hand, and went and sat on top of the mountain, and began to chip small stones away from it. Some people came by and asked him: What are you doing? He said to them: I am going to uproot the mountain and throw it into the Jordan! They said to him: You cannot uproot the entire mountain! But he kept hacking away, until he came to a big boulder. So, he wedged himself underneath it, pried it loose, and threw it into the Jordan. And he said to it: Your place is not here,

Avot D'Rabbi Natan - Chapter 6

but there! This is what Rabbi Akiva did to Rabbi Eliezer and Rabbi Tarfon. Rabbi Tarfon said to him: Akiva, it is about you that the verse says, "He stops up the streams so that hidden things may be brought to light." For Rabbi Akiva has brought to light things, which are kept hidden from human beings.

Every day, he would bring a bundle of sticks, half of which he would sell to support himself and half he would use for kindling. His neighbours came and said to him: Akiva, you are choking us with all this smoke. Sell it all to us instead, and then buy oil with the money, and study by the light of a candle. He said to them: But I take care of many of my needs with it. I study by its light. I warm myself by its fire. And then I can make it into a bed and sleep on it.

All the poor will one day be judged against Rabbi Akiva, for if one says to them: Why did you never study? And they say: Because we were poor! Then we will say to them: But wasn't Rabbi Akiva even poorer, completely impoverished? And if they say: It is because of our babies, we will say: But didn't Rabbi Akiva have sons and daughters as well? But they will say: It is because he merited to have his wife Rachel to help him.

He was forty years old when he went to study Torah, and after thirteen years, he was teaching Torah to the masses. It was said that he did not leave the world until he had tables full of silver and gold, and he could go up to his bed on golden ladders. His wife would go out in a fancy gown and with golden jewellery with an engraving of Jerusalem on it. His students said: Rabbi, you are embarrassing us with what you have done for her. He said to them: She suffered greatly with me for the sake of Torah.

Avot D'Rabbi Natan - Chapter 6

What were the origins of Rabbi Eliezer ben Hyrcanus? He was twenty-two years old and he had never studied Torah. One day he said: I will go and study Torah with Rabbi Yohanan ben Zakkai. His father, Hyrcanus, said to him: You will not eat until you have plowed a full plot of ground. He got up and plowed a full plot of ground. It is said that it was Friday, and so he went and ate with his father-in-law. But some say that he ate nothing from six hours before the Sabbath until six hours after the Sabbath. When he was on the road, he saw a stone that looked like food and he took it and put it in his mouth. And some say that it was cow dung. He went and spent the night in an inn. Then he continued on, until he came before Rabbi Yohanan ben Zakkai in Jerusalem. Soon Rabbi Yohanan noticed Eliezer's terrible breath. Rabbi Yohanan said: Eliezer, my son, have you eaten anything today? Eliezer said nothing. Rabbi Yohanan asked again and again; Eliezer said nothing. He sent a message to the inn, asking: Did Eliezer eat anything when he stayed with you? They replied: We thought perhaps he would be eating with the rabbi. He said: I, likewise, thought perhaps he had eaten with you. Meanwhile, between our two assumptions, we ended up neglecting Eliezer. So, Rabbi Yohanan said to Eliezer: Just as you have had this terrible smell coming from your mouth, so will you one day have a great reputation from the Torah coming from you.

His father, Hyrcanus, heard that he had gone to study Torah with Rabbi Yohanan ben Zakkai. He said to himself: I will go and force Eliezer to swear off any claim to my property. It is said that on that day, Rabbi Yohanan was sitting and interpreting Torah in Jerusalem, and all the great minds of Israel were sitting before him. He heard that Hyrcanus had come, and he spoke to the guards

Avot D'Rabbi Natan - Chapter 6

and said: If he tries to sit here, do not let him. He did try to sit, and they did not let him. So, he went up several rows until he found a place near Tzitzit ben HaKeset, Nakdimon ben Gurion, and Kalba Savua. He sat down next to them, nervously. It is said that on that day, Rabbi Yohanan ben Zakkai looked at Rabbi Eliezer and said: Open our session with an interpretation. He replied: I cannot open. Rabbi Yohanan and the other students pressured him until he stood up and opened with an interpretation that no ear had ever heard before. At every word that came out of his mouth, Rabbi Yohanan ben Zakkai would stand up and kiss him on the head and say to him: Eliezer, my rabbi, you have taught me truth!. Before the gathering ended, Hyrcanus stood up and said: Gentlemen, I came here in order to have my son swear off any claim to my property. But now all of my property will be given to my son Eliezer, and all his brothers will get nothing!.

And why was that man called "Tzitzit HaKeset"? Because he would lean on a silver bed at the head of all the great minds of Israel.

They say about the daughter of Nakdimon ben Gurion that her bed was worth twelve thousand gold dinars, and that she would spend a gold dinar every week on cooking spices, and that she was waiting for levirate marriage.

And why was he called "Nakdimon ben Gurion"? Because the sun once came out nakdah for his sake. Once, the Jews were going up to Jerusalem for a festival, and they did not have water to drink. Nakdimon ben Gurion went up to a gentile general and said: Lend me the rights to twelve springs of water from now until a certain date in the future, and if I do not give you back twelve springs worth of water, I will give you twelve bars of silver. So

Avot D'Rabbi Natan - Chapter 6

they set a date. When the time came, the general sent a messenger, saying: Send me either the twelve spring's worth of water or the twelve bars of silver. He replied: Wait, the day has still not ended. The general laughed at him and said: What, all year there has been no rain, and today you expect rain to fall? The general then went off to the bathhouse, quite pleased with himself. Nakdimon ben Gurion went to the study hall, wrapped himself in a prayer shawl, and stood in prayer and said: Master of the World, you know well that it is not for my own honor that I did this, nor for the honor of my father's house, but only for Your honor, so that there would be water for those going up to the festival. Immediately, the sky filled with clouds and it began to rain so hard that it filled all twelve springs of water and then some. He sent a message to the general, saying: Send me money for the extra water you now have. The general replied: The sun has already set and the water that has fallen is now in my property. He went back to the study hall, wrapped himself in his prayer shawl, and stood in prayer and said: Master of the World, make a miracle for me at the end of the day as you did at the beginning. Immediately, the wind blew and the clouds parted, and the sun was shining. The two met and the general said to Nakdimon: Now I know that the Holy Blessed One does not disturb the order of the world except for your sake.

And why was he called "Kalba Savua"? Because anyone who went into his house as hungry as a dog kelev would come out of his house satiated save'a. And when the emperor Vespasian came to destroy Jerusalem, the Zealots wanted to burn everything good in it to the ground. Kalba Savua said to them: Why do you want to destroy this city and burn everything good in it to the

Avot D'Rabbi Natan - Chapter 6

ground? Wait here for me and I will go in my house and show you what I have. He went in and found that he had enough grain to feed everyone in Jerusalem for twenty-two years. He immediately ordered that they pile it up, sift it, grind it, refine it, knead it, bake it, and prepare food for everyone in Jerusalem for twenty-two years. But the zealots would not listen to him. So, what did the people of Jerusalem do? They brought calves and dragged them into pens, and then would grind them up in the mud, and the people of Jerusalem would also boil straw and eat it. Those who were positioned on the walls of Jerusalem would say: If someone will give me five dates, I will go down and take five heads from Vespasian's men. Vespasian examined their excrement and saw that there was no grain in it and said to his soldiers: These people who are eating nothing but straw are still killing you! If they could eat and drink all that you do, imagine how many more of you they would have killed!

Avot D'Rabbi Natan - Chapter 7

Chapter 7

Yosef ben Yohanan, a man of Jerusalem, would say: Let your house be open to all, let the poor be members of your household, and do not talk too much with married women.

Let your house be open to all. How so? This teaches that a person's house should be open to all sides: the south, the east, the west, and the north. This is like Job, who made four doors to his house. Why did Job make four doors to his house? Therefore, the poor would not have to trouble themselves to go around the whole house. Someone who came in from the north would enter from that direction, and someone who came in from the south would enter from that direction, and so with every direction. That is why Job made four doors to his house.

Let the poor be members of your household. Not that they will be actual members of your household, but they will speak of what they ate and drank in your house, in the way that they speak of what they ate and drank in the house of Job. For when they would meet, one would say to another: Where are you coming from? And the other would reply: From the house of Job; and where are you going? And the first one would say: "To the house of Job."

So, when all the great tragedies came upon him, Job said before the Holy Blessed One: Did I not feed the hungry and give drink to the thirsty? As it says, "Did I ever eat my food alone, and not let orphan eat from it?" And did I not clothe the naked? As it says, "He warmed himself from the shearing's of my sheep." And even so, these tragedies came upon me. The Holy Blessed One said to Job: Job, you still have not gotten to even half the level

Avot D'Rabbi Natan - Chapter 7

of Abraham. You sit and wait in your house, and guests come in to you. And if it is someone's custom is to eat wheat bread, you feed him wheat bread. And if someone's custom is to eat meat, you feed him meat. And if someone's custom is to drink wine, you pour him wine. But Abraham did not do this. Rather, he sat and looked out at the world, and when he would see potential guests, he would go bring them into his house. And if someone was not accustomed to eating wheat bread, he would feed him wheat bread. And if someone was not accustomed to eating meat, he would feed him meat. And if someone was not accustomed to drinking wine, he would pour him wine. Not only that, but he built large booths out on the roads, where he would leave food and drink, and anyone who came by and entered would eat and drink and bless the heavens, and he would feel content. Anything that one could ask for was available in the house of Abraham, as it says, "And he planted an Eshel tree in Beer Sheba."

Teach the members of your household humility. When a person is humble and the members of his household are humble, then when a poor person comes to the door of his house and asks: Is your father home? They will say: Yes, come in. And before he even enters, a table will be set before him, and he can go right in and eat, and drink, and bless in the name of Heaven, and feel a great sense of contentment. But when a person is humble but the members of his household are unkind, then when a poor person comes to his door and asks: Is your father home? They will say to him: No, and scold him harshly, and drive him out.

Another interpretation of "Teach the members of your household humility": How so? When a person is humble and the members of his household are humble, then when

Avot D'Rabbi Natan - Chapter 7

he travels to faraway country, he says: I am grateful to you, the Eternal, my God, that my wife is not making trouble with others, and his heart is not anxious, and his mind is settled. But when a person is not humble and the members of his household are unkind, then when he travels to a faraway country, he says: May it be your will, the Eternal, my God, that my wife not make trouble with others and that my children not start fights, and his heart is anxious and his mind is not settled until he returns.

And do not talk too much with married women. That is, even with his own wife, not to mention with his friend's wife. For when a person talks too much with married women, he brings evil upon himself, neglects the words of Torah, and in the end will be doomed to Gehinnom.

Another interpretation of Do not talk too much with married women: How so? When a person comes to the study hall and they do not treat him with respect, or he has a fight with his friend, he should not go and tell his wife: I fought about this and that with my friend, and he said this and that to me, and then I said this and that to him. For in doing so, he disgraces himself and disgraces his wife and disgraces his friend. And his wife, who had treated him with respect, will now begin to ridicule him. And when his friend hears, he will say: Oy! Those things were between him and me, and he went and told them to his wife. So it is that this man has disgraced himself, and his wife, and his friend.

Avot D'Rabbi Natan - Chapter 8

Chapter 8

Yehoshua ben Perachya and Nittai the Arbelite received from them. Yehoshua ben Perachya said: Make for yourself a teacher, and acquire for yourself a friend, and judge everyone favorably.

Make for yourself a teacher. How so? This teaches that one should make a regular relationship with his teacher, and should learn from him Scripture, Mishnah, Midrash, Halakhot, and Aggadot. The explanation for what he has learned in Scripture will eventually be told to him in Mishnah. And the explanation for what he has learned in Midrash will eventually be told to him in the Halakhot. And the explanation for what he has learned in the Halakhot will eventually be told to him in the Aggadah. And so this person will come to be settled in his place and full of goodness and blessing.

Rabbi Meir would say: Someone who learns Torah from one teacher – what is he like? Like someone who had one field and planted part of it with wheat and part of it with barley and part of it with olives and part of it with trees. We find such a person is full of goodness and blessing. But when someone learns from two or three teachers, he is like someone who has many fields. One he plants with wheat and one he plants with barley and one he plants with olives and one he plants with trees. We find such a person is spread out across the land, and is without goodness or blessing.

And acquire for yourself a friend. How so? This teaches that a person should acquire a friend for himself who will eat with him, and drink with him, and study Scripture and Mishnah with him, and go to sleep with him, and tell him all his secrets, both secrets of the Torah and secrets of the

Avot D'Rabbi Natan - Chapter 8

ways of the world: For when they sit and engage in Torah together, and one of them makes a mistake in the law, or the division of chapters, or declares an impure thing pure, or a pure thing impure, or a forbidden thing permitted or a permitted thing forbidden, then his friend will correct him. And how do we know that when his friend corrects him and studies with him, that they will have great reward from their studies? For it says, "The two are better than the one, for they have great reward from their efforts."

When three people sit and engage in Torah together, the Holy Blessed One considers it as if they had become one unified troop before Him, as it says, "Who built His chambers in the heavens, and founded His troop on earth. Who summons the water to the sea and spills it out on the face of the earth. the Eternal is His name." From this you learn that three who sit and engage in Torah are regarded as if they had become a unified troop before the Holy Blessed One.

When two people sit together and engage in Torah, their reward is accrued on High – as it says, "Then the God-fearing people spoke together, every man to his fellow, and the Eternal listened." And who are these God-fearing people? It is those who make a public proclamation, saying: We must go and release prisoners and redeem the captives. Then the Holy Blessed One provides for them and they are able to go and accomplish this immediately. And who are those that "think of God's name"? These are the people who just think silently in their hearts: We should go and release the prisoners and redeem the captives. The Holy Blessed One does not provide for them, and an angel comes along and smacks them to the ground.

Avot D'Rabbi Natan - Chapter 8

When one person sits alone and engages in Torah, his reward is accrued on High, as it says, "Let him sit alone in silence, for God has placed it upon him." They gave a parable: To what can this be compared? It can be compared to someone who had a young son whom he left alone and went out to the marketplace. The boy went and got a scroll and placed it on his knees, and was sitting and studying it when his father came back from the marketplace. The father said: Look at my young son whom I left alone when I went to the marketplace! What did he do? He took it upon himself to study, and he went and got a scroll and placed in on his knees and sat and studied it! You learn from this that even one person who sits alone and engages in study accrues his reward on High.

And judge everyone favourably. There is a story of a young woman who was kidnapped, and two pious men went to pay her ransom. One of them went into a brothel. When he came out, he said to his friend: What did you suspect when you saw me go in there? He replied: Only that you were trying to find out what her ransom would be. He said: That is in fact what happened. And just as you judged me favourably, so the Holy Blessed One will judge you favourably."

There is another story of a young woman who was kidnapped, and two pious men went to pay her ransom. One of them was arrested and accused of robbery and sent to prison. Every day, his wife would bring him bread and water. One day, he said to her: Go to my friend the other pious man and tell him that I am being held in prison and accused of soliciting a prostitute, while he just sits in his house and does nothing to help the young woman. His wife replied: It's bad enough that you are being held in

Avot D'Rabbi Natan - Chapter 8

prison, but now you also engage in this kind of foolishness? He said to her: Please, just go and say this to him. So, she went and related this to his friend. What did the friend do? He went and brought silver and gold, and other men with him, and got them both released. When the first man got out, he said: Let me sleep next to the young woman in bed, but with her clothes on. In the morning, he said to them: Now immerse me in water, and then immerse her in water. They did so. Then he said to them: What did you suspect during my immersion? They said to him: We said to ourselves, all that time that he was in prison, he was hungry and thirsty, and now he is out in the fresh air… ….so this all warmed up your flesh and you were over stimulated, so perhaps you had an ejaculation and that is why you had to immerse. He said: And what did you suspect during her immersion? They said to him: After all that time that she was among the idolaters, perhaps she ate and drank from their foods, and now you were telling us to immerse her so that she would be purified. He said to them: That is in fact just what happened, and you, who have judged me favourably, will be judged favourably by the Omnipresent God.

The early righteous people were pious, so too were their animals. They say that Abraham's camels would not go into a house that had idols in it, as it says, "I have cleared the house, and made space for the camels." I have cleared the house - Of idols. What do you learn from "and made space for the camels"? That teaches us that they would not go into the house of Lavan the Aramean until all the idols were cleared out.

There is a story that Rabbi Hanina ben Dosa's donkey was stolen by robbers. They put it in the courtyard and placed straw, barley, and water in front it, but it would

Avot D'Rabbi Natan - Chapter 8

not eat or drink. They said: How can we leave it here? It will just die and rot in the courtyard. So, they opened the door and put the animal outside, and it started walking and kept going until it reached the home of Rabbi Hanina ben Dosa. When it got there, his son heard it braying. He said: Father, isn't this voice is like the voice of our animal? He said: Son, open the door for it, for it is clearly dying of hunger. He got up and opened the door, and put straw and barley and water in front of it, and it ate and drank. That is why they say: Just as the early righteous people were pious, so too were their animals."

Avot D'Rabbi Natan - Chapter 9

Chapter 9

Yehoshua ben Prachya and Nittai the Arbelite would say: Stay away from a bad neighbor, do not befriend the wicked, and do not think there is no punishment.

Stay away from a bad neighbor. Whether a neighbor in your house, a neighbor outside, or a neighbor in the field. This teaches us that afflictions come only upon the house of the wicked, as it says, "A wicked person will be trapped by his sins." This teaches us that afflictions come only for the sins of the wicked. But the sins of the wicked cause him to knock down the wall of the righteous. If there is a wall between a wicked person and a righteous person, and an infestation appears in the house of the wicked one on the wall that stands between him and the righteous one, they will end up knocking down the wall] of the righteous one for the sins of the wicked. Rabbi Yishmael the son of Rabbi Yohanan ben Beroka would say: Woe to the wicked, and woe to his neighbor for the sins of the wicked cause them to knock down the wall of the righteous.

Our ancestors tested the Holy Blessed One ten different times, but they were punished only for the sin of slander which was one of them. These are the ten: Once at the sea, once when the manna was first given, once when the manna stopped coming down, once at the first appearance of quails, once at the latter appearance of quails, once at Marah, once at Refidim, once at Horev, once at the Calf, and once] with the spies. And the sin of the spies was the worst of them all, as it says, "They have tested me these ten times, and have not heeded my voice." And also, "The men died before God by plague, for spreading bad reports about the Land of Israel." And from this we can reason

Avot D'Rabbi Natan - Chapter 9

that if the Holy Blessed One punished the spies for insulting the land, which has no mouth to speak, no reaction, and no shame, then all the more so would the Holy Blessed One punish someone who speaks ill of his friend and shames him.

Rabbi Shimon would say: Afflictions come upon those who speak slander. For so we find with Aaron and Miriam, who spoke slanderously about Moses, and punishments came upon them – as it says, "Miriam and Aaron spoke against Moses." And why does the verse place Miriam before Aaron? This teaches us that Tzipora the wife of Moses went and talked to Miriam, and then Miriam went and told everything to Aaron, and then the two of them began to speak against this righteous man. And because these two spoke against a righteous man, punishments came upon them, as it says, "And the Eternal became angry with them, and departed." What do we learn from "and departed"? This teaches us that God departed from Aaron and attached to Miriam, because Aaron was not as engaged as Miriam in spreading slanderous words around, so she was immediately punished more. Miriam said: Prophecy has come to me even though I have not separated from my husband. And Aaron said: Prophecy has come to me even though I have not separated from my wife. And even our earliest ancestors received prophecy even though they did not separate from their wives. But Moses, because he is so arrogant, separated from his wife. They did not take this up with Moses directly, nor did they know for certain that it was true. It was not at all clear that he was being arrogant. We can reason from this that if Miriam, who spoke against her brother only secretly, was still

Avot D'Rabbi Natan - Chapter 9

punished, then if one speaks against his friend publicly, and shames him, all the more so will he be punished.

At that time, Aaron said to Moses: Moses, my brother, you think that this skin disease affects only Miriam, but it is also upon the flesh of our father Amram. I will give you a parable to tell you what this is like: Like someone who has a hot coal placed in his hand. Even if he tosses it around from place to place, his flesh is still burned." This is why it says, "Please, do not let her be like one who is dead when she emerges from her mother's womb, with half of her flesh eaten away." Meanwhile, Aaron attempted to pacify Moses by saying: Moses, my brother, have we ever done harm to anyone in the world? He replied: No. Aaron continued: So, if we have done no harm to anyone in the world, would we have wished to harm you, who are our brother? Now what can I do? Will this mistake come between the covenant between us? For he had established a covenant with Aaron and his sons, as it says, "They did not remember the covenant of brotherhood." At that moment, Moses drew a small circle on the ground and stood inside it, and asked for mercy for Miriam. He said: I will not leave this spot until my sister Miriam is healed, as it says, "Please, God, heal her." Then the Holy Blessed One said to Moses: If a king had reprimanded her, or if her father had reprimanded her, it would have been appropriate for her to sit in shame for seven days. And since it is I, the King of all kings, all the more so is it just for her to sit in shame for fourteen days! However, for your sake, I will forgive her, as it says, "The Eternal said to Moses: If her father spat in her face would she not sit in shame for seven days?"

"Moses was a very humble man". Could it be that he was meek and not beautiful and praiseworthy? But we learn

Avot D'Rabbi Natan - Chapter 9

from the verse, "He spread the tent over the Tabernacle": That just as the Tabernacle was ten cubits high, so was Moses also ten cubits high. Could it be that he was as humble as the angels, who serve God? But we learn from that same verse that Moses was humble "more than any other person"; more than other people, that is, but not more than the angels who serve God. Could it be that he was humbler than those in previous generations? But we learn from that same verse, "on the face of the earth"; in his generation, that is, and not previous generations. There are three types of skin-afflicted people in the world: moist, dry, and polypous, and Moses made himself lowlier than them all.

Rabbi Shimon Ben Elazar would say: Afflictions come upon those who speak slanderously. This is what you see with Gehazi, who slandered his teacher and was afflicted with a skin disease that clung to him until the day he died, as it says, "May the skin disease of Na'aman cling to you…and he left him, and he was flaky like the snow."

He would also say: Afflictions come upon the arrogant. This is what we find with Uzziah, as it says, "And when King Uzziah became strong, his heart became so proud that he became corrupt, and trespassed against the Eternal his God by entering the Temple of the Eternal to offer incense on the altar. And after him came] the priest Azariah, with eighty other brave priests of the Eternal. They stood up against King Uzziahand said to him: It is not for you, Uzziah, to offer incense to the Eternal, but for the priests, who are the descendants of Aaron, who have been consecrated, to offer incense. Get out of the Sanctuary, for you have trespassed, and there will no glory for you from the Eternal God. Uzziah, holding the incense lighter, became angry; but as he became angry

Avot D'Rabbi Natan - Chapter 9

with the priests, a skin disease broke out on his forehead." At that moment, the Temple split apart into two halves, twelve miles apart. The priests, panicking, rushed to get out, "and he, too, rushed to get out, for the Eternal had afflicted him. And he was a leper until the day he died. He stayed in isolated quarters, as a leper, and he was cut off from the House of the Eternal, while Jotham his son was put in charge of the king's house, and governed the people of the land".

Do not befriend the wicked. This teaches us that a person should not befriend a bad person, or a wicked person. For so we find with Jehoshafat, that he befriended Ahab and went up with him to Ramot Gilad, and the Eternal's rage came out upon him. Then he befriended Ahaziah and they made ships in Etzion Gever, and the Eternal destroyed his work, as it says, "'Because you have befriended Ahaziah, the Eternal will destroy your work,' and so the ships were broken up." And so, too, we find with Amnon, who befriended Jonadab, who then gave him bad advice, as it says, "Amnon had a friend named Jonadab, son of David's brother Shim'ah; and Jonadab was a very wise man" – that is, wise in the ways of wickedness. Another interpretation of Do not befriend the wicked: Even to study Torah.

Do not think there is no punishment. How so? This teaches us that a person's heart should be fearful every day and he should say: Woe is me! Perhaps punishment will come upon me today, or perhaps tomorrow. So he ends up being fearful every day], as it says in Job, "I have feared and feared."

Another interpretation of Do not think there is no punishment: How so? When a person sees that he is successful, he should not say: Because I deserve it, the

Avot D'Rabbi Natan - Chapter 9
Omnipresent God has given me food and drink in this world as interest, and the principal will remain for me in the World to Come. Rather, he should say: Woe is me! Perhaps I have only one good deed to show for, and so God has given me food and drink in this world in order that I will lose all reward in the World to Come."

Avot D'Rabbi Natan - Chapter 10

Chapter 10

Yehudah ben Tabbai and Shimon ben Shetach received from them. Yehudah ben Tabbai would say: Do not act as an advocate for one side, and when the litigants stand before you, you should consider them both guilty; but when they depart from you, you should consider them both innocent, for they have accepted the judgment upon themselves.

Do not act as an advocate for one side. How so? This teaches that if you came to the house of study and heard a general teaching or a legal teaching, do not respond immediately. Rather, sit and ask about the reasoning behind their teaching, and in what context they made such a judgment. To the one who gave the legal teaching, ask first about the legal principle and the timing of the case. When two litigants come before you for judgment, one poor and one rich, do not say to yourself: How can I make sure to exonerate the poor one and charge the rich one? Or how can I exonerate the rich one and charge the poor one? For if I charge the poor one, then he will become my enemy, but if I exonerate the poor one, then the rich one will become my enemy. And do not say to yourself: How can I take this one's money and give it to that one? For the Torah says, "Do not be partial in judgment."

Rabbi Meir would say: What do we learn from this: "Hear out low and high alike"? That one person should not be made to stand while the other one sits, or one person be allowed to talk as much as he wants while the other is told to be brief. Rabbi Yehudah said: I heard that if the judges want to seat both litigants at once, they may do so; it is not forbidden. And what is forbidden? That one person sits and one stands. Rather, what do we learn from "Low

Avot D'Rabbi Natan - Chapter 10

and high alike"? That the judgment of the lowly be just the same for you as the judgment of the exalted, and the judgment of a perutah be just the same to you as the judgment of a hundred manah.

He would say: If anyone had said to me before I entered this position: Enter! I would have threatened his life. Now that I have entered it, if anyone would say to me: Step down! I would want to throw a pot of boiling water on him. For greatness is difficult to attain. But just as it is difficult to attain, so is it difficult to let go of. And so, we find with Saul, when they said to him: Assume the kingship! He hid from it, as it says I, "The Eternal said: Look, he is hiding among the baggage." But when they said to him: Step down! He went after David and tried to kill him.

Shimon Ben Shetach would say: Investigate the witnesses thoroughly. But while you are investigating them be careful with what you say, for they may hear your words and figure out how to add lies to them.

Avot D'Rabbi Natan - Chapter 11

Chapter 11

Shemaya and Avatalyon received from them. Shemaya would say: Love work, hate power, and do not become too familiar with the authorities.

Love work." How so? This teaches us that a person should love work, and not hate work. For just as the Torah was given in a covenant, so work was given in a covenant, as it says, "For six days you shall labor and do all your work, and the seventh day is the Sabbath of the Eternal your God." Rabbi Akiva would say: Sometimes a person labors and escapes death, and sometimes a person does not labor and becomes liable for death from Heaven. How so? Say a person sat around all week and did no labor, and then on the eve of the Sabbath he had nothing to eat. But he had money that had been designated to the Temple in his house. So, he took from this and ate, and thus became liable to death from Heaven. However, if he had labored on the building of the Temple, then even though they paid him in money designated for the Temple and he took that money and used it for food, he would still escape the death penalty.

Rabbi Dostai would say: How do we know that if someone did no work all six days, he will end up doing work on the seventh? For, see, if he sat all the days of the week and did no work, and then on the eve of the Sabbath he had nothing to eat, he would then go out looking, and end up seized by conscription officers, who would grab him by the collar and force him to do on the Sabbath all the work that he did not do for six days.

Rabbi Shimon Ben Elazar would say: Even Adam did not taste anything until he worked, as it says, "And God placed him in the garden, to work it and guard it"; and

Avot D'Rabbi Natan - Chapter 11

then it says, "From every tree of the garden you may certainly eat."

Rabbi Tarfon would say: Even the Holy Blessed One did not rest His presence upon Israel until they had done work, as it says, "Make Me a Sanctuary, and I will dwell among them."

Rabbi Yehudah Ben Beteira would say: If someone who has no work to do, what should he do? If he has a dilapidated yard or field, he should go and work on them, as it says, "Six days you shall labor and do all your work." What do we learn from the phrase, "do all your work"? That even someone who has dilapidated yards or fields should work on them.

Rabbi Yosei HaGalili would say: A person dies only because of idleness, as it says, "And he expired or: exhausted himself, and so was gathered to his people." And see, if someone is pushed and falls over on his own craftwork and dies, we know his death was because of idleness. And if he was standing on the top of the roof, the top of a palace, or the top of any building, or at the edge of the river, and he fell and died, we know his death was because of idleness.

All this we know to be true for men. And how do we know it is also true for women? For it says, "Let no man or woman do any more work for the donations to the Sanctuary." And how do we know it is true also for children? For it says, there, "So the people stopped bringing."

Rabbi Natan said: When Moses was carrying out the work of the Tabernacle, he did not want to take direction from the chiefs of Israel. So, the chiefs of Israel sat there quietly and said: Perhaps now Moses will need our help. When they heard the announcement in the camp that said

Avot D'Rabbi Natan - Chapter 11

enough work had been done, they said: Alas, we have not participated at all in the work of the Tabernacle! So, they got up and added a great thing by themselves, as it says, "And the chiefs brought the shoham stones for the breastplate of the high priest."

Hate power. How so? This teaches that a person should not place a crown on his own head. But others can place it upon him, as it says, "May a stranger praise you, but not your own mouth; a foreigner, but not your own lips." Rabbi Akiva said: Anyone who raises himself above the words of Torah is like a carcass cast off on the side of the road. Everyone who passes it sits down and puts his hand out to check for breath, and then backs away from it and leaves, as it says, "If you degrade yourself with arrogance, and if you scheme, a hand to your mouth." Ben Azzai said: Learn this idea out of the verse itself: If a person degrades himself for words of Torah by eating rotten dates, and dressing in filthy clothes, and sitting and watching at the door of the sages, then all who pass by will say, "Perhaps he is an idiot." But in the end, you will find that he has the whole Torah with him. Rabbi Yosei would say: Anyone who raises himself above the words of Torah, in the end they will debase him; but anyone who debases himself for the sake of the words of Torah, in the end they will elevate him.

Do not become too familiar with the authorities. How so? One's name should not be known to the authorities. For when one's name is known to the authorities, they will eventually take notice of him, and kill him and take his money. How so? While in the marketplace, someone says about his friend: May the Holy Blessed One bless so-and-so, who as of today has on his property a hundred bulls, a hundred lambs, and a hundred goats. But an official

Avot D'Rabbi Natan - Chapter 11

overhears this and goes and tells the magistrate, who goes and surrounds the friend's property and takes all his money. About him Scripture says, "One who blesses his friend too loudly...a curse is accounted to him."

Another interpretation of Do not become too familiar with the authorities: If one's friend is in the marketplace and says: May the Holy Blessed One give to so-and-so, who as of today has on his property several bundles of wheat and several bundles of barley, but robbers overhear him, and come and surround his property and take all of his money, come morning he will have nothing. About him Scripture says, "One who blesses his friend loudly etc."

Another interpretation of Do not become too familiar with the authorities: How so? This teaches us that a person should not intend to say: I will become the magistrate of the city, or his second-in-command. For these people rob Israel.

Another interpretation: A person should not seek authority, even though in the beginning they arrange all kinds of benefits for him, for in the end they will set him with up all kinds of difficulties.

Avtalyon would say: Sages! Be careful with your words. Perhaps people will teach things in your name that are not in accordance with the proper study of Torah. Then you will come to deserve exile, and be exiled to a place of poisoned waters. And then even the students who come after you may teach something in your names that is not in accordance with the proper study of Torah, and then you will have caused them to deserve exile, and they will be exiled to a place of poisoned waters. And what are these poisoned waters? This is what is spoken of, "They will become mixed up among the nations, and they will

Avot D'Rabbi Natan - Chapter 11

learn their ways." Others say that the term poisoned waters are to be taken literally. And there are those who say that perhaps it means hard labor.

Avot D'Rabbi Natan - Chapter 12

Chapter 12

Hillel and Shammai received from them. Hillel would say: Be like the students of Aaron: Love peace, and pursue peace, and bring peace between one person and another, and between husband and wife, love all people, and bring them closer to Torah. He would also say: One, who pursues a name, loses his name. One, who does not increase, diminishes. One, who does not learn, deserves to die. One, who makes use of the crown, passes away.

He would also say: If I am not for myself, who will be for me? And when I am only for myself, what am I? And if not now, when?

Love peace. How so? This is to teach you to be a person who loves peace among all the people of Israel, just as Aaron loved peace between everyone, as it says, "A Torah of Truth was on his mouth, and no crooked thing was on his lips. He walked with me in peace and righteousness, and he pulled back many from sin."

Rabbi Meir would say: What do we learn from "he pulled back many from sin"? When Aaron was walking down the road, and he came upon a wicked person, he would wish him Shalom. The next day, when that man wanted to sin, he would say: Alas! How will I be able to look Aaron in the face; I will be so embarrassed when he wishes me Shalom. And so, this man would stop himself from sinning.

Similarly, when two people were fighting with one another, Aaron would go and sit next to one of them and say: My son, look at the anguish your friend is going through! His heart is ripped apart and he is tearing at his clothes. He is saying how can I face my old friend? I am so ashamed; I betrayed his trust. Aaron would sit with

Avot D'Rabbi Natan - Chapter 12

him until his rage subsided. Then Aaron would go to the other person in the fight and say: My son, look at the anguish your friend is going through! His heart is ripped apart and he is tearing at his clothes. He is saying, how can I face my old friend? I am so ashamed; I betrayed his trust. Aaron would sit with him until his rage subsided. When the two people saw each other, they would embrace and kiss one another. And that is why it says, "And the entire House of Israel wept for Aaron for thirty days" after his death.

Another interpretation: Why did Israel weep for Aaron for thirty days? Aaron had always judged fairly. How do we know this? For he never said to a man or woman: You have disgraced yourself. That is why it says that the entire House of Israel wept for him. But with Moses, who would chastise them with harsh words, it merely says, "The children of Israel wept for Moses." And also, how many thousands in Israel were named after Aaron! If not for Aaron, they would never have come into the world. He would bring peace between husband and wife, and then they would come back together, and would name their first child after him. But there are those who say that the reason the entire House of Israel wept for him for thirty days is because anyone who saw Moses our teacher sitting and weeping, how could they not weep? And some say: Anyone who saw Elazar and Pinchas, the two high priests, standing and crying, how could they not weep?

At that time, Moses asked to die as Aaron had died, because he saw the great honor Aaron was given at the funeral procession, with rows and rows of angels eulogizing him. But did he actually say this to someone? No, he just said it to himself. Yet the Holy Blessed One heard his whisper, as it says, "And you will die on the

Avot D'Rabbi Natan - Chapter 12

mountain that you go up on, and be gathered to your people, just as your brother Aaron died on Mount Hor." From this you learn that he asked to die as Aaron had died.

At that time, God said to the Angel of Death: Go, bring me the soul of Moses. The Angel of Death went and stood before him, and said: Moses, give me your soul. But he scowled at him and said: The place I sit, you have no right to even stand – and you ask me to give you my soul? So, he scowled at him and chased him away with a rebuke.

The Holy Blessed One said again to the Angel of Death: Go, bring me the soul of Moses.

Finally, the Holy Blessed One said to Moses: Moses! You've had enough of this world. The World to Come has been prepared for you since the six days of creation. As it says, "God said, here is a place near me; stand on that rock." The Holy Blessed One took Moses' soul and stored it under the Throne of Glory. As it says, "And the soul of my master will be bound up in the bond of life.") And when He took it, He did it with a kiss. As it says, "Moses died... by the mouth of God." And not only Moses' soul is stored under the Throne of Glory, but also the souls of all the righteous are stored there! As it says, "If anyone sets out to pursue you and seek your life, the soul of my master will be bound up in the bond of life." Could it be that the souls of the wicked are there, too? The verse continues: "but He will fling away the lives of your enemies like a slingshot." To what can this be compared? It can be compared to someone who takes a stone and places it in a sling; even though he flings it from place to place, he does not know where it will land. So it is for the souls of the wicked, which cast about and go wandering the world, and have no place to rest.

Avot D'Rabbi Natan - Chapter 12

The Holy Blessed One said again to the Angel of Death: Go, bring me the soul of Moses. He went back to the place, and looked for Moses, but could not find him. He went to the Great Sea and said to it: Did Moses come here? And it said: I have not seen him since the day that Israel passed through me. He went to the mountains and hills and asked them: Did Moses come here? They said to him: We have not seen him since the day that Israel received the Torah on Mount Sinai. He went down to the Underworld and to Oblivion said to them: Did Moses come here? They said: We have heard his name, but we have never seen him. He went and asked the angels: Did Moses come here? They said to him: God knows his path and his place. God stored him away for the World to Come, and no living creature knows where. As it says, "Where will wisdom be found, and where is the place of understanding? No human knows its measure, and it cannot be found in the land of the living. The Deep says, it is not in me, and the sea says it is not by me... .... Oblivion and Death say: in our ears we heard a rumor." Even Joshua was sitting in despair over Moses for he did not know where he was, until the Holy Blessed One said to him: Joshua, why are you in despair over Moses? For "Moses My servant is dead.".

Pursue peace. How so? This teaches that a person should pursue peace in Israel between everyone in the way that Aaron would pursue peace in Israel between everyone, as it says, "Turn from evil and do good; seek peace and pursue it."

Rabbi Shimon Ben Elazar would say: If a person stays quietly in his place, how can he pursue peace in Israel between everyone? Rather, he should go out from his place and into the world and pursue peace in Israel, as it

Avot D'Rabbi Natan - Chapter 12

says, "Seek peace and pursue it." How does this work? Seek it where you are, and pursue it in some other place. Even the Holy Blessed One made peace in the heights, for He did not call ten angels Gabriel, ten angels Michael, ten angels Uriel, and ten angels Raphael, in the way humans do, calling ten people Reuben, ten people Shimon, ten people Levi, and ten people Judah. For if He had done as humans do, when He called one of them, they all would have come, and then become jealous of one another. So instead, He called only one angel Gabriel and one Michael, and when He calls any one of them, that angel comes before Him, and He dispatches the angel wherever He desires. And how do we know that they revere one another, and respect one another, and are humbler than human beings? Because when they open their mouths to sing a song, one of them says to the other: You should begin, for you are greater than I, and then the other one says: No, you should begin, for you are greater than I. This is not the way it is with human beings. Every person says to another: I am greater than you, and the other person responds: No, I am greater than you.

And some say they spoke in groupings of angels. One grouping would say to the other: You all should begin, for you are greater than we, as it says, "And this one called out to that one and said...."

Love all people. How so? This teaches us that a person should love all people and not hate anyone. For so we find with the people of the Generation of the Dispersion, that because they loved one another, the Holy Blessed One did not want to wipe them off the face of the earth, but instead only scattered them to the four corners of the world. But the people of Sodom, because they hated one another, the Holy Blessed One took them out of both this

Avot D'Rabbi Natan - Chapter 12

world and the World to Come, as it says, "And the people of Sodom were very wicked and sinful against God." "Sinful" – this is sexual transgression; "against God" – this is the desecration of God's name; "very" – this means that they sinned intentionally. From this you learn that because they hated one another, the Holy Blessed One took them out of both this world and the World to Come. And bring them closer to Torah. How so? This teaches us that a person should prevail upon others and bring them under the wings of the Divine Presence, just as Abraham prevailed upon those around him and brought them under the wings of the Divine Presence. And not only Abraham, but also Sarah, as it says, "Abram took his wife Sarai, and his nephew Lot, and all of their possessions, and the souls they had made in Haran." But even if everyone in the world got together, they would be unable to create even one mosquito! So, what does it mean when it says, "the souls they had made in Haran"? It teaches us that the Holy Blessed One considered it as if they had actually made new souls.

When a person does not give part of what he earns to his fellows in this world, then he will not be given anything in the World to Come, as it says, "Look at the tears of the oppressed, and they have no comforter. Power is in the hand of their oppressors, and they have no comforter." Why does it say "they have no comforter" twice? This refers to people who eat and drink in this world, and their sons and daughters are successful, but in the World to Come they have nothing and they have no comforter. For if a person has something stolen from him in this world, or if someone he knows dies, then his children, siblings, and other relatives come and comfort him. Could it be that the same is true in the World to Come? That is why

Avot D'Rabbi Natan - Chapter 12

the verse then says, "He has neither son nor brother."

So, too, with someone whose sexual transgression produces a mamzer a child born of certain forbidden sexual relations they say to him: Empty one! You have ruined yourself and you have ruined him as well! For this mamzer would have wanted to study Torah with the rest of the students who sit and study in Jerusalem. But this mamzer would go with them only up to Ashdod, and then would stop there and say: Woe is me! If I were not a mamzer, I would have gone to sit and study among the students whom I have been studying with until now. But because I am a mamzer, I cannot sit and study among these students. For a mamzer cannot enter Jerusalem at all, as it says, "The mamzer will stay in Ashdod, and I will cut off the pride of the Philistines."

Hillel would also say: If I am not for myself, who will be for me? That is, if I do not earn merit during my lifetime, who will earn it for me? And when I am only for myself, what am I? That is, if I do not earn merit for myself, who will earn my merit for me? If not now, when? That is, if I do not earn merit during my lifetime, who will earn if for me after my death? And so, it is said, "For a living dog is better off than a dead lion." "A living dog is better off" – this refers to a wicked person who is still alive in this world. "Than a dead lion" – he is better off than even Abraham, Isaac, and Jacob, for they lie in the dirt. Another interpretation of "a living dog is better off": This refers to a wicked person who is still alive in this world; if he repents, then the Holy Blessed One will receive it. But when a righteous person has died, he can no longer add to his merit.

He would also say: If you come to my house, I will come to your house. My legs will bring me to the place that my

Avot D'Rabbi Natan - Chapter 12

heart loves.

If you come to my house, I will come to your house. How so? These are the people who come for the morning and evening prayers at the synagogues and study houses. The Holy Blessed One blessed them in the World to Come. This is like what it says, "In every place where I have my name mentioned I will come to you and bless you."

My legs will bring me to the place that my heart loves. How so? These are the people who leave their silver and gold and go up to the festival to encounter the face of the Divine Presence in the Temple. The Holy Blessed One will protect them in their encampments, as it says, "No man will covet your land when you go up to appear before the face of the Eternal your God, on one of the three pilgrim festivals."

He would also say: If I am here, everything is here. I am not here, who is here? Turn it over, and turn over in it. For everything is in it. And in all matters, the reward is in proportion to the struggle.

There is a story of Hillel the Elder, which he was walking on the road, and he came upon people who were carrying wheat. He said to them: How much would a se'ah cost? They said to him: Two dinars. He came upon another group, and asked them: How much would a se'ah cost? They said to him: Three dinars. He said: But the first group told me it was only two! They said to him: You stupid Babylonian! Don't you know that the reward is in proportion to the struggle? He said them: You fools! And empty ones! Because I constantly instruct you that the reward is commensurate with the toil, you are replying so in kind? Thus, Hillel the Elder did to them to bring them back to good behavior.

It was also he who saw a skull floating on the water and

Avot D'Rabbi Natan - Chapter 12

said to it: Since you drowned others, you were drowned. And those who drowned you will also be drowned.

He also used to teach four things in the Babylonian tongue: One who pursues a name, loses his name; One who does not serve the sages, deserves death; One who does not increase, loses; and One who makes use of the crown, perishes, and then it is lost to him.

One, who pursues a name, loses his name. How so? This teaches us that a person should not seek to be known in the state, for eventually they will begin to take note of him, and then kill him and take his money.

He, who does not serve the sages, deserves death. How so? They tell There is a story about a person from Beit Ramah who conducted himself with great piety. Rabban Yohanan ben Zakkai sent one of his students to go check up on him. The student went, and found him putting oil on a stovetop, and then taking it off and putting it on beans. The student said to him: What are you doing? He replied: I am a high priest, and I am eating the priestly tithe in a state of ritual purity. The student said: But is that stovetop impure or pure? He said: Does it say anywhere in the Torah that a stovetop can be impure? The Torah speaks only of an oven becoming impure, as it says, "Everything in it becomes impure." The student replied: Just as the Torah speaks of an oven becoming impure, so it speaks also of a stovetop becoming impure, as it also says, "An oven and a stovetop must be smashed; they are impure." And if that is so, you have never eaten the priestly tithe in a state of purity in your entire life!

He, who does not add, loses. How so? This teaches us that if a person learns only one tractate – or even two, or three – but does not keep adding to them, in the end he will forget even those he did learn.

Avot D'Rabbi Natan - Chapter 12

He, who uses it as a crown, perishes, and then it is lost to him. How so? For anyone who uses the Ineffable Name of God has no share in the World to Come.

Avot D'Rabbi Natan - Chapter 13

Chapter 13

Shammai would say: Make your Torah study a fixed practice, say little and do a lot, and greet everyone with a smile.

Make your Torah study a fixed practice. How so? This teaches us that if a person hears advice from the mouth of a sage in the study hall, he should not make it an occasional practice but a fixed practice. What a person learns, he should do, and then teach others, and they should do, as it says, "Learn them, and take care to do them." And also, in Ezra it says, "For Ezra had prepared his heart to seek the Torah of the Eternal and to do it." And after that, it says, "and to teach Israel rules and laws."

Say little and do a lot. How so? This teaches us that the righteous say little and do a lot, but the wicked say a lot and don't do anything at all. And how do we know that the righteous say little and do a lot? For this is what we find with Abraham our forefather, who said to the angels, "Have a piece of bread with me today," as it says, "I will get a piece of bread, and you can dine to your heart's content." But then after that, look at what Abraham did for the angels who serve God! He went and prepared three bulls and nine measures of fine flour for them! And how do we know that he prepared nine measures of fine flour? Because it says, "Abraham hurried into the tent, to Sarah, and said: Hurry! Three measures of fine flour! The word three refers to the first three measures, the word fine brings it to six, and the word flour makes nine. And how do we know that he prepared three bulls for them? Because it says, "Abraham ran to the cattle and selected a good, tender calf." Cattle are one bull. Calf is two.

Avot D'Rabbi Natan - Chapter 13

Tender are three. And some say that good was four. "Then he gave it to the boy, who hurried to prepare it." That is, he gave it to Ishmael, in order to train him in performing the mitzvot.

Even the Holy Blessed One said little and did a lot, as it says, "God said to Abram: Know well that your offspring will be strangers in a land not their own, and they shall be enslaved and oppressed for four hundred years. But I will judge the nation that they serve, and afterward they shall go out with great wealth." God spoke of this judgment with only the two letters dalet and nun, which spell the word dan - judge. But when the time came to pay back the enemies of Israel, God used seventy-two letters to do it, as it says, "Or has any god attempted to come and take one nation out from another, with great acts, signs, and wonders, and with awesome power?" From this you learn that when the enemies of Israel were made to pay for what they had done, they paid with seventy-two letters.

And how do we know that the wicked say a lot and don't do anything at all? For this is what we find with Ephron, who said to Abraham, "A piece of land worth four hundred pieces of silver; what is that between you and me?" For if he was willing to give away the land for free. But in the end, when Abraham went to give him the payment, it says, "Abraham understood Ephron, and paid him the money" and he simply accepted it.

Greet everyone with a smile. How so? This teaches that if a person gives his friend all the finest gifts in the world, but does so with a pained face, Scripture considers it as if he had given him nothing. But one who receives his friend with a smile, even if he gives him nothing, Scripture considers it as if he had given him all the finest gifts in the world.

Avot D'Rabbi Natan - Chapter 14

Chapter 14

Rabban Yohanan ben Zakkai received from Hillel and Shammai. Hillel the Elder had eighty students. Thirty of them were worthy of having the Divine Presence rest upon them like Moses our teacher; it was only that their generation was not fit for it. Thirty of them were able to make adjustments to the calendar. And twenty of them were average.

The greatest of them all was Yonatan Ben Uziel and the lowest of them was Rabban Yohanan Ben Zakkai. And they said about Yohanan Ben Zakkai that he was not ignorant of anything: Scripture; Mishnah; Talmud, including Halakhot, Aggadot, and all kinds of other material; grammatical analysis of the Torah; analysis of the scribal traditions; and all the interpretive traditions of the sages. He did not leave aside anything in the Torah, in order to fulfill the words, "I give substance to those who love me; I will fill their treasuries."

He would also say: If you have achieved greatness in Torah, do not give yourself the credit; it was for this purpose that you were created. For all things were created in order to be involved in Torah.

Rabban Yohanan Ben Zakkai had five students, and he had a name for each of them. He called Eliezer Ben Hyrcanus "the Plastered Pit," because it never loses a drop, and "the Sealed Bottle," because it keeps all of its wine. He called Yehoshua Ben Hananya "the Triple Knot," because it does not get severed easily. He called Yosei Ha Kohen "the Saint of the Generation." He called Yishmael Ben Hananya "the Oasis in the Desert," which holds on to its water. Happy is the student whose teacher praises him and speaks of his virtues! He called Elazar

Avot D'Rabbi Natan - Chapter 14

Ben Arach "the Flowing Stream" and "the Bubbling Brook," for its waters overflow and go out into the world, as it says, "Your wellsprings will burst forth, and the streams will spill out onto the streets."

He would also say: If all the sages of Israel were on one end of a scale and Rabbi Eliezer Ben Hyrcanus was on the other end, he would outweigh them all. But Abba Shaul says in Rabban Yohanan Ben Zakkai's name: If all the sages of Israel were on one end of a scale, and Rabbi Eliezer Ben Hyrcanus was with them, but Rabbi Elazar Ben Arach was on the other end – he would outweigh them all.

He said to them: Go out and see what is the best path that a person should stay on, so that he can follow it into the World to Come. Rabbi Eliezer came back and said: A good eye. Rabbi Yehoshua came back and said: A good friend. Rabbi Yosei came back and said: A good neighbor, good desires, and a good wife. Rabbi Shimon said: One who sees what is coming. Another version says: Like Mordechai the Jew, who saw what was coming. Rabbi Elazar came back and said: A good heart toward Heaven, and a good heart toward others. Rabban Yohanan Ben Zakkai said to them: I prefer Rabbi Elazar Ben Arach's words, because I see all of your words contained within his words.

He said to them: Go out and see: What is the evil path that a person should stay away from so that he can enter into the World to Come. Rabbi Eliezer came back and said: An evil eye. Rabbi Yehoshua came back and said: An evil friend. Rabbi Yosei came back and said: An evil eye, an evil neighbor, and an evil wife. Rabbi Shimon came back said: One who borrows money and does not pay it back. For one who borrows from people will be punished by

Avot D'Rabbi Natan - Chapter 14

God, as it says, "The wicked one borrows and does not repay; the righteous one is generous and keeps giving." Rabbi Elazar came back and said: An evil heart toward Heaven, an evil heart toward the mitzvot, and an evil heart toward others. Rabban Yohanan ben Zakkai said to them: I prefer Rabbi Elazar Ben Arach's words, because I see all of your words contained within his words.

When Rabban Yohanan Ben Zakkai's son died, his students came in to comfort him. Rabbi Eliezer came in and sat before him and said: My master, if you please, may I say something? He said: Speak. So, he said: Adam the first person had a son who died and he accepted comfort. And how do we know that he accepted comfort? It says, "And Adam knew his wife again." So, you, too, should accept comfort. He replied: Is it not enough that I have my own pain but that you need to remind me of Adam's pain as well?

Rabbi Yehoshua came in and said to him: If you please, may I say something before you? He said: Speak. So, he said: Job had sons and daughters, and they all died on the same day, and he accepted comfort. So, you, too, should accept comfort. And how do we know that Job accepted comfort? For it says, "The Eternal has given, and the Eternal has taken away. Blessed is the name of the Eternal." He replied: Is it not enough that I have my own pain but that you have to remind me of Job's pain as well?

Rabbi Yosei came in and sat before him and said: My master, if you please, may I say something? He said: Speak. So, he said: Aaron had two older sons and they both died on the same day, and he accepted comfort, as it says, "And Aaron was silent," and silence always indicates comfort. He replied: Is it not enough that I have my own pain but that you have to remind me of Aaron's

Avot D'Rabbi Natan - Chapter 14

pain as well?

Rabbi Shimon came in and said: My master, if you please, may I say something? He said: Speak. So, he said: King David had a son who died, and he accepted comfort. So, you, too, should accept comfort. And how do we know that David accepted comfort? For it says, "David comforted his wife Bath Sheba, and he came to her and lay with her, and she gave birth to another son, and called him Solomon." So, you, too, should accept comfort. He replied: Is it not enough that I have my own pain but that you have to remind me of King David's pain as well?

Rabbi Elazar Ben Azariah came in. When Rabbi Yohanan saw him, he said to his steward: Take this vessel, and follow me to the bathhouse, because this is a great man, and I will not be able to withstand him. So, Rabbi Elazar came in and sat before Rabbi Yohanan and said: Let me give you a parable. To what can this be compared? It can be compared to a person to whom the king gave a deposit to hold. Every day he would cry and scream and say, Oy, when will I be free of this deposit? So, it is with you, Rabbi. You had a son who read from the Torah, the Prophets and the Writings; the Mishnah; Halakhah; and Aggadah; and then was taken from the world free of sin. Must you, then, accept consolation when you have returned a deposit whole? He said: Rabbi Elazar, my son, you have comforted me as people are supposed to.

When they all left, Elazar said: I am going to Damasit, a beautiful place with good, sweet water. They said: We will go to Yavneh, a place where there is an abundance of scholars who love the Torah. So, he went to Damasit, the beautiful place with good, sweet water, and his reputation in Torah study diminished. And they went to Yavneh, the place where there was an abundance of

Avot D'Rabbi Natan - Chapter 14
scholars who all loved the Torah, and their reputations in Torah study grew.

Avot D'Rabbi Natan - Chapter 15

Chapter 15

They said three things. Rabbi Eliezer said: Your friend's honor should be as dear to you as your own. Do not be easy to anger. Repent one day before your death.

Your friend's honor should be as dear to you as your own. How so? This teaches us that one should regard his friends honor just as he regards his own. Just as no one wants to have a bad reputation, likewise one should not want anyone to tarnish his friend's reputation.

Another interpretation: Your friend's honor should be as dear to you as your own. How so? When someone has a hundred thousand, and all his money is taken from him, he should not degrade himself for a small coin.

Do not be easy to anger. How so? This teaches us that a person should always be humble like Hillel the Elder, and not severe like Shammai the Elder.

And what was the humility of Hillel the Elder? It once happened that two men made a wager with each other, saying: Whoever can make Hillel angry shall receive four hundred zuz. One of them went off to try. It was the Sabbath eve near sundown, and Hillel was washing the hair on his head. The man went, passed by the door of his house, and called out: Where is Hillel? Where is Hillel? Hillel dressed and went out to him, saying: My son, what do you need? I have a question to ask, said he. Hillel replied, Go ahead. So, he asked: Why are the eyes of the Tarmudim so narrow? Hillel replied: Because they live in sandy places and the wind comes and blows it into their eyes. Therefore, their eyes have narrowed. The man left, waited a while, returned, knocked on the door, and called out: Where is Hillel? Where is Hillel? Hillel dressed and went out to him, saying: My son, what do you need? I

Avot D'Rabbi Natan - Chapter 15

have a halachic legal question to ask, said he. Hillel replied, Go ahead. So, he asked: Why are the feet of the Africans so wide? Hillel replied: Because they live in watery marshes, and every day they have to walk through water. Therefore, their feet have become wide. The man left, waited a while, returned, knocked on the door, and called out: Where is Hillel? Where is Hillel? Hillel dressed and went out to him, saying: What do you need to ask? The man replied: I have to ask a halachic question. Go ahead, said Hillel, and he wrapped himself in his robe and sat down before him. So, the man asked: Why are the heads of the Babylonians so pointy? Hillel replied: My son, you have asked a great question. It is because they have no skillful midwives there. So, when a baby is born, the servants just yank them out with their hands. That is why their heads are so pointy. But here, where there are skilled midwives, when a baby is born, they place it in a cradle and massage its head. That is why their heads are round!

Then the man said: I have lost four hundred zuz through you! Hillel replied: Hillel is worth your losing four hundred zuz, and yet another four hundred zuz through him – yet Hillel will not lose his temper!

What was the severity of Shammai the Elder? They say that once a person came before Shammai and asked him: Rabbi, how many Torahs do you have? Two, he replied, the Written Torah and the Oral Torah. The man said to him: I believe you with respect to the Written Torah, but not with respect to the Oral Torah. Shammai scolded him and kicked him out angrily. He went before Hillel, and asked him: Rabbi, how many Torahs do you have? Two, he replied, the Written Torah and the Oral Torah. The man said to him: I believe you with respect to the Written

Avot D'Rabbi Natan - Chapter 15

Torah, but not with respect to the Oral Torah. Hillel said: My child, sit down and write for me the alphabet. Hillel said: What is this? The man said: An aleph. Hillel said: No, that's not an aleph, it's a beit. Then he said: And what is this? The man replied: That's a beit. No, that's not a beit, it's a gimmel, said Hillel. Hillel continued: Tell me, from where do you know that this one is an aleph and this one is a beit? The man replied: This is what our ancestors passed down, that this is an aleph, and this a beit, and this a gimmel. Hillel said: Just as you have accepted that faithfully, so accept this faithfully.

On another occasion, a foreigner was passing behind a synagogue, when he heard a child reciting the verse, "And these are the garments which they shall make; a breastplate and an ephod." So, he went before Shammai and said to him: For whom is all this honor? Shammai answered: For the high priest, when he is performing his service on the altar. So, he said: Convert me, but only on the condition that you make me the high priest. Shammai replied: Do we not have priests in Israel? Do we not already have a high priest who will serve us? Do we need some convert who has come with his staff and his knapsack to serve as the high priest? So, he scolded him and kicked him out angrily.

He then went before Hillel, and said: Convert me, but only on the condition that you appoint me the high priest, so I can go up and serve on the altar. Hillel said: Sit down, and I will tell you something. If someone wants to appear before a human king, isn't it necessary that he learn how to make his entrance and exit? Yes, the man replied. Hillel continued: So, you, who wish to appear before the King of all kings, the Holy Blessed One, how much more necessary for you to learn how to enter the Holy of

Avot D'Rabbi Natan - Chapter 15

Holies, how to light the lamps, how to come close to the altar, how to order the table, and how to prepare the fire on the altar! The man then replied: Tell me what you think is the best way to do this. So, Hillel wrote for him the alphabet, and he learned it. Then he gave him the book of Leviticus, and he continued learning the rest of the Torah until he came to the verse, "The Levites shall set up the Tabernacle, and any stranger who comes close shall die." The convert reasoned: If Israel, who are called children of the Omnipresent, and of whom the Shekhinah said, "And you shall be to Me a kingdom of priests and a holy nation," and even so they were so warned by this verse that "any stranger who comes close shall die," then how much more so I, a mere convert, who has come with only his knapsack! And the convert was immediately at peace with this. He came to Hillel the Elder and said: May all the blessings that are contained in the Torah come upon your head. Had you been like Shammai the Elder, I would not have come into the congregation of Israel. His severity nearly caused me to be lost both in this world and in the World to Come; but the humility of Hillel has brought me to a life in this world and in the World to Come. It was said that this convert had two sons. He named one Hillel and the other Gamliel, and they were called Hillel's converts.

Repent one day before your death. How so? Rabbi Eliezer's students asked him: But does a person know what day he will die, so that he could repent? He said to them: All the more so should he repent every day, for perhaps he will die the next day! And the result is that he repents all of his days! Rabbi Yosei bar Yehudah said in the name of Rabbi Yehudah son of Rabbi Ilai, who said this in the name of his father Rabbi Ilai, who said it in the

Avot D'Rabbi Natan - Chapter 15

name of Rabbi Eliezer the Great, repent one day before your death, and warm yourself before the fire of the sages, but be careful not to get burned by their coals. For, their bite is like the bite of a fox, and their sting is like the sting of a scorpion, and all of their words are like fiery coals.

Avot D'Rabbi Natan - Chapter 16

Chapter 16

Rabbi Yehoshua would say: The Evil Eye, the Evil Urge, and the hatred of others take a person out of the world. The Evil Eye, How so? This teaches that a person should regard his friend's household just as he regards his own household. Therefore, just as a person does not want people to say disparaging things about his wife and children, so he should not want people to say disparaging things about his friend's wife and children. Another interpretation: The Evil Eye. How so? A person should not look askance at his friend's learning. There is a story of someone who looked askance at his friend's learning, and his life was cut short, and he reached his end prematurely and passed on from the world.

The Evil Urge. How so? They say that for the first thirteen years of a person's life the Evil Urge is greater than the Good Urge. There in his mother's womb, a person's Evil Urge grows with him. After he emerges into the world, he starts breaking the Sabbath, and nothing is there to stop him; killing people and nothing is there to stop him; going out to sin, and nothing is there to stop him.

After thirteen years, the Good Urge is born. Then when he breaks the Sabbath, it says to him: Empty one! Isn't it written, "One who breaks it will surely die"? When he kills, it says to him: Empty one! Isn't it written, "One who spills the blood of a person, his own blood will be spilled"? When he goes out to sin, it says to him: Empty one! Isn't it written, "Both the adulterer and the adulteress shall be put to death"?

When a person heats himself up, and then goes to commit some act of lewdness, all of his limbs will obey him, because the Evil Urge rules over all 248 limbs. When he

Avot D'Rabbi Natan - Chapter 16

goes to perform a mitzvah, his limbs begin to grow lazy, because the Evil Urge in his stomach rules over all 248 of a person's limbs. The Good Urge, meanwhile, is like someone trapped in a prison, as it says, "From the prison, he comes forth to rule" – that is the Good Urge.

Some say, that verse refers to Joseph the Righteous, when that wicked woman came and tortured him with words. She said to him: I will lock you up in prison! He said to her: But God releases the bound. She said to him: I will poke out your eyes! He said: God gives sight to the blind. She said to him: I will bend you down! He said to her: God straightens the bent. She said to him: I will make you into a wicked man! He said to her: God loves the righteous. She said to him: I will make you an Aramean! He said to her: God protects the strangers. Until finally he said, "How can I do this evil thing?"

And do not be surprised at Joseph the Righteous. For behold, Rabbi Tzadok was the greatest of his generation when he was captured. And a matron took him and presented before him a beautiful maidservant. When he saw her, he turned his eyes to the wall so he would not see her. And he sat and recited his learning the whole night. In the morning, the maidservant left and complained to her mistress: I would rather die than be given to that man! The matron sent for him and said to him: Why didn't you do with this woman as all people do? He said to her: What can I do? I come from the lineage of the high priest, from a great family! I said to myself, Perhaps I will sleep with her and increase mamzerim in Israel! When she heard this, she commanded he be released with great honor. And they say: Do not be surprised at Rabbi Tzadok. For behold, Rabbi Akiva was greater than him! When he went to

Avot D'Rabbi Natan - Chapter 16

Rome, informers slandered him to a local prefect, who then presented before him two beautiful women. The prefect bathed and anointed them dressed them up like brides, and they fell upon Rabbi Akiva the whole night. This one said: Come to me! And that one said: Come to me! But he sat between them and spat, and would not turn to them. They went before the prefect and said to him: We would rather die than be given to that man! He sent for Rabbi Akiva and said to him: Why didn't you do with those women as all people do with women? Weren't they beautiful? And weren't they human beings just like you? Didn't the One who created you create them as well? Rabbi Akiva said: What could I do? Their scent was worse to me than carcasses and vermin! And do not be surprised at Rabbi Akiva. For behold, Rabbi Eliezer the Great was greater than him. He raised his sister's daughter until she was thirteen years old. She slept in bed with him until she began puberty. Then he said to her: Go, and marry a man. She said to him: Am I not your woman? Should I be given as a maidservant to wash the legs of your students? He said to her: My daughter, I am already an old man. Go and marry a young man like yourself. She said to him: Didn't I already say to you, Am I not your woman? Should I be given as a maidservant to wash the legs of your students? When he heard her words, he got permission from her to marry her, and then had sexual relations with her.

Rabbi Reuven Ben Itzrubali would say: How can a person stay away from the Evil Urge inside of him? For the first drop that a person puts inside of a woman is the Evil Urge. The Evil Urge rules only over the doors of the heart, as it says, "Sin crouches at the door." From the first moment that an infant is placed in the crib, this man is

Avot D'Rabbi Natan - Chapter 16

trying to kill you. He wants to pluck you out by your hair. When an infant is placed in his crib, he will place his hand onto a snake or a scorpion's stinger. It is the Evil Urge inside of him that causes him to do this. He will place his hand onto fiery coals and it will be burned. It is the Evil Urge inside of him that causes him to do this. For the Evil urge wants to throw him into the fire. But look at a baby goat or sheep! When they see a well, they back up away from it, because there is no Evil Urge in an animal.

Rabbi Shimon Ben Elazar would say: I will give you a parable. What is the Evil Urge like? The Evil Urge is like a piece of steel that they put into the fire. While it is in the fire, they can make any tool they wish from it. So, it is with the Evil Urge. There is no way to fix it except with words of Torah alone which are like fire, as it says, "If your enemy is hungry, feed him bread. If he is thirsty, give him water. You will be heaping fiery coals on his head, and the Eternal will reward you." Do not read it as "reward you" yeshalem lekha but "give you peace" yashlim lekha.

Rabbi Yehudah HaNasi would say: I will give you a parable: What is the Evil Urge like? The Evil Urge is like two people who go into an inn. One is captured by robbers. They say to him: Who is with you? He could easily say: No one else was with me. But he says to himself: Since I am going to be killed, my friend should be killed with me. So it is with the Evil Urge, which says: Since I will be lost in the World to Come, I want take the whole body with me!

Rabbi Shimon Ben Yochai would say: From this you know that Israel will never see the face of Gehenna. They give a parable: To what can this be compared? It can be compared to a human king who had a barren field. Some

Avot D'Rabbi Natan - Chapter 16

people came along and rented it for ten bundles of wheat. They fertilized it, plowed it, watered it, and harvested it, but they yielded only one bundle of wheat the whole year. The king said to them: What is this? They said: Our master the king, you know that with regard to the field you gave us, in the beginning you were not able to yield anything from it. Now we have fertilized it, harvested it, and watered it, yet we have still not been able to yield more than one bundle of wheat the whole year. So will Israel say one day before the Holy Blessed One: You know well that the Evil Urge has tempted us, as it says, "For He knows our urges" [lit., how we were formed].

Hatred of Others, How so? This teaches that a person should not say: Love the sages, but hate the scholars; or: Love the scholars, but hate the common people. Rather, love all of them, but hate the heretics, the enticers, the bad influences, and the traitors. So, too, did David say, "I will hate those who hate You, O Lord, and I will despise those who rise up against you. With the utmost hatred I will hate them. They will become my enemies." But it also says, "You shall love your neighbor as yourself; I am the Eternal." What is the reason? Because I created him. So, if he does well by you, you should love him. And if not, you should not love him.

Rabbi Shimon Ben Elazar would say: This was meant as a great oath. "You shall love your neighbor as yourself; I am the Eternal." I created him, so if you love him, I can be relied upon to give you great reward. And if not, I am the judge who will punish you.

Avot D'Rabbi Natan - Chapter 17

Chapter 17

Rabbi Yosei would say: Let your friend's money be as precious to you as your own. And set a plan for yourself to study Torah, because it does not simply come to you as an inheritance.

How so? This teaches that just as a person sees his own money, so should he see his friend's money. And just as a person does not want people to speak badly about his finances, so should he not want people to speak badly about his friend's finances.

Another interpretation of Let your friend's money is as precious to you as your own: How so? When a student enters your house and says: Teach me, if you are able to teach him, teach him; if not, release him immediately, and do not take his money, as it says, "Do not say, Go, and come back tomorrow, and I will give it to you, when you have it on you."

Set a plan for yourself to study Torah. How so? When Moses our teacher saw that his children were not learned enough in Torah, to be able to rise to leadership after him, he wrapped himself up and arose to pray. He said before God: Master of the World! Let me know who should come in and go out as the head of this people, as it says, "Moses spoke to the Eternal, saying, Let the Eternal, the God of the spirits of all flesh, appoint a man over the congregation who will go out before them and come in before them." The Holy Blessed One replied to Moses: Moses, take Joshua for yourself. Then the Holy Blessed One said to Moses: Go and find a disseminator for him, and have him give a teaching at the head of the great men of Israel. Immediately, Moses said to Joshua: Joshua, these that I turn over to you are not goats but kids, and

Avot D'Rabbi Natan - Chapter 17

not sheep but lambs. For they still have not taken on the mitzvot. They still have not become fully grown goats, as it says, "If you do not know, most beautiful of women, go out and follow the footsteps of the flock, and graze your kids by the shepherd's dwellings."

Once, Rabbi Yohanan ben Zakkai was walking through the marketplace and he saw a young woman who was collecting barley from under the legs of the animals of the Arabs. He said to her: My daughter, who are you? She was quiet. He said again: My daughter, who are you? She was quiet. Then she said to him: Wait one moment. She wrapped herself with her hair and sat in front of him and said: Rabbi, I am the daughter of Nakdimon Ben Gurion. He said to her: So, my daughter, where is all your father's money? She said: Rabbi isn't it like what they say in Jerusalem: One who wants to preserve his fortune must give some of it up. Or, as some say, must be kind. He said to her: And what about your father-in-law's household? She replied: One lost the fortunes of the other. Then Rabban Yohanan Ben Zakkai said to his students: All my life, I have read this verse - from Song of Songs, "If you do not know, most beautiful of women, go out and follow the footsteps of the flock, and graze your kids by the shepherd's dwellings." But I did not understand that there was a punishment in it until what I saw today. Now I see that Israel will be punished by subjugation to a lowly nation and not only to a lowly nation, but to the dung droppings of their animals. Again, she spoke to him and said: Rabbi, do you remember that you signed my marriage contract? He said: Yes. Then he said to his students: It is true that I signed this young woman's marriage contract, which was worth a million golden Tyrian dinars. Her father's family would not leave their

Avot D'Rabbi Natan - Chapter 17

house to enter the Temple unless a woolen rug was laid out for them.

There is another story of a young woman who was captured – she and her ten maidservants, and a Samaritan took her and brought her up in his house. One day, he gave her a jug and said to her: Go out and fetch me some water. One of her maidservants got up and took the jug from her. The man said to the maidservant: What is this? She said: Master, I swear on your head, I was one of five hundred maidservants that this young woman's mother had! When he heard these words, he freed the young woman and her ten maidservants.

There is yet another story of a young woman who was captured, and a Samaritan took her and brought her up in his house. A dream interpreter came to him and said: Let this young woman go out of your house. But his wife said: Do not let her go! The dream interpreter came again and said to him: If you do not let this woman go, I will kill you! So, he went and let her go. But he followed after her, saying: I will go and see what will become of this young woman. As she was walking along the road, she became thirsty and went down to drink water from a spring. When she placed her hand on the wall, a snake came out and bit her, and she died and began to float on the water. So, he went down, and took her, and brought her up and buried her. He came back and said to his wife: This nation that you see suffers only the wrath of their Father in heaven.

Let all your actions be for the sake of Heaven. Meaning, for the sake of Torah, as it says, "In all your ways, know God, and He will straighten out your paths."

Rabbi Shimon would say: Be careful when you say the Shema and your prayers. And when you pray, do not make your prayer just a regular conversation, but a deep

Avot D'Rabbi Natan - Chapter 17

pleading before the Holy Blessed One, as it says, "For You are a gracious and compassionate God, slow to anger, full of kindness and forgiving punishment." Rabbi Eliezer would say: Be diligent in studying Torah, and know how to respond to a heretic, and do not forget one word of Torah. Know before whom you labor and with whom you have made your covenant, and know that He can be trusted to reward you for your actions.

Avot D'Rabbi Natan - Chapter 18

Chapter 18

Rabbi Yehudah HaNasi would praise the virtues of these sages: Rabbi Tarfon, Rabbi Akiva, Rabbi Elazar Ben Azariah, Rabbi Yohanan Ben Nuri, and Rabbi Yosei HaGalili.

He called Rabbi Tarfon: a pile of stones. And some say, a pile of nuts. For when someone pulls one of them out, they all fall down and crash in on each other. So, it was with Rabbi Tarfon. When a student would come before him and say: Teach me something; Rabbi Tarfon would cite Scripture, Mishnah, Midrash, Halakhot, and Aggadot. And the student would leave feeling full of goodness and blessing.

He called Rabbi Akiva: a sealed vault. Rabbi Akiva was like a worker who took his basket and went out to gather. When he found wheat, he put it in his basket. When he found barley, he put it in his basket. When he found spelt, he put it in his basket. When he found beans, he put them in his basket. When he found lentils, he put them in his basket. Then when he came back home, he would separate the wheat into one pile, the barley into one pile, the spelt into one pile, the beans into one pile, and the lentils into one pile. So, it was with Rabbi Akiva. He organized the whole Torah into identifiable categories.

He called Rabbi Elazar Ben Azariah: a spice-peddlars' basket. For Rabbi Elazar was like a merchant who took his cart and traveled around the country, and everyone would come out and say to him: Do you have fine oil? Do you have herbal ointments? Do you have persimmons? And they would find that he had everything. So, it was with Rabbi Elazar Ben Azariah. When a student would come to him and ask a question, Rabbi Elazar would tell

Avot D'Rabbi Natan - Chapter 18

him something from Scripture, something from Mishnah, something from Midrash, something from the law, and something from the legends. And the student would leave feeling full of goodness and blessing.

When Rabbi Yehoshua was very old, his students came to visit him. He said to them: My children! What new teachings did you come up with in the house of study? They said to him: We are your students, and we drink from your waters. He said to them: God forbid! This is not a generation without sages! Whose turn was it to speak on the Sabbath? They said: It was Rabbi Elazar Ben Azariah's Sabbath. He said to them: And what was the subject of the day? They said: The commandment to "gather the whole nation; the men, the women, and the babies" for a public Torah reading. He said to them: And what did he speak about? They said to him: This is what he said: The men come to learn, and the women come to hear. But why must the babies come? In order to reward those who bring them. He said to them: You had this pearl of wisdom in your hands, and you wanted to keep it from me? If you had come today only to teach me that one thing, it would have been enough! They said: He also taught about the verse, "The words of the sages are like goads, like nails fixed in herding sticks." Just as a goad is used to direct a cow to her furrow, so do words of Torah direct a person toward the paths of life. And lest you think that just as a goad is movable, so words of Torah are easily moved around, it says, "like nails fixed," to tell you that just as something fixed cannot be uprooted, so too, words of Torah cannot be uprooted. "Herding sticks" refers to the scholars, who gather together to sit in packs. Now, these may prohibit something, and these may permit it; these may say something is impure, and these

Avot D'Rabbi Natan - Chapter 18

may say it is pure; these may say something is invalid, and these may say it is valid. And so perhaps someone will say: I give up! One cannot learn anything! That is why it says at the end of the verse, "all given from one shepherd." One God created them. One leader – Moses, transmitted them. And the Master of all Things said them: As for you, make your ear like a funnel and take in the words of those who prohibit and the words of those who permit, the words of those who say "impure" and the words of those who say "pure," the words of those who invalidate and the words of those who validate.

And he called Rabbi Yohanan Ben Nuri: a bundle of laws. And he called Rabbi Yosei HaGalili: a collector of beautiful things, with no arrogance in him. For he took ahold of the spirit of the sages from Mount Sinai, and taught it to all the sages of Israel.

Isi Ben Yehudah had names for the sages. He called Rabbi Meir: A sage and a scribe. He called Rabbi Yehudah: A sage in whatever field he wishes to be. He called Rabbi Eliezer Ben Ya'akov: A small vessel, but airtight. He called Rabbi Yosei: The one with the explanation. He called Rabbi Yosei HaGalili: A collector of beautiful things, but beauty without any pride. He called Rabbi Shimon Ben Gamliel: A shop filled with regal fineries. He called Rabbi Shimon: Learns a lot, forgets a little.

After this, Rabbi Shimon found Isi Ben Yehudah and said to him: Why have you insulted my learning before the scholars? He replied: All I said was that you learn a lot and forget a little, and whatever you forget is irrelevant to the learning.

Avot D'Rabbi Natan - Chapter 19

Chapter 19

Akavia Ben Mehalelel would say: Anyone who takes these four things to heart will never sin again: Where he comes from, where he is going, what he will become, and who his judge is. Where does he come from? He comes from a place of darkness. Where is he going? To a dark and cloudy place. What will he become? Like Dirt, worms, and maggots. And who is his judge? The King of all kings, the Holy Blessed One.

Rabbi Shimon would say: He comes from a place of darkness, and returns to a place of darkness. He comes from a disgusting drop, from a place that the eye cannot see. And what will he become? Dirt, worms, and maggots, as it says, "How much less the human – a worm, the person – a maggot." Rabbi Elazar Ben Ya'akov would say: A worm in his life, and a maggot in his death. How is he a worm in his life? Because lice and maggots infests him in his death, and they crawls upon him when he is dead.

Rabbi Shimon Ben Elazar would say: I will give you a parable. To what can this be compared? It can be compared to a king who built a great palace and took residence there. There was a gutter filled with animal skins from a tannery that passed right by the entrance to the palace. So, everyone who walked by and sat there would say: How beautiful and impressive this palace is! If only there wasn't a smelly gutter that passed right by! So, too, is the human being. If he is so proud of himself now, when a disgusting stream comes out of his innards, just think how arrogant he would be if he could somehow produce a stream of fine oil, persimmons, and herbal ointments!

Avot D'Rabbi Natan - Chapter 19

When Rabbi Eliezer became sick, his students came to visit him, and they sat before him and said to him: Rabbi, teach us one of the things you've taught us before. He said to them: What shall I teach you? Be careful to treat one another with respect. When you are praying, know before whom you stand. By doing this, you will merit life in the World to Come. Rabbi Elazar Ben Azariah said: We learned about the status of five things from Rabbi Eliezer, and we took even greater joy from the knowledge after he passed away than we had while he was alive. And they are: a circular cushion, a ball, a mannequin, an amulet, and a torn prayer box. We asked: What is their status? He replied: They are impure, and he told us to be careful with them, and dip them in water. For these are established laws that were told to Moses on Mount Sinai.

Avot D'Rabbi Natan - Chapter 20

Chapter 20

Rabbi Hananya, deputy of the priests, would say: Anyone who takes words of Torah to heart is no longer troubled by thoughts of destruction, thoughts of hunger, foolish thoughts, lustful thoughts, thoughts of temptation, thoughts of another man's wife, thoughts of meaningless things, or thoughts of human burden. So, it was written in the book of Psalms by King David, "The precepts of the Eternal are true, bringing joy to the heart. The commandments of the Eternal are clear, illuminating the eyes." But anyone who does not take words of Torah to heart is troubled by thoughts of destruction, thoughts of hunger, foolish thoughts, lustful thoughts, thoughts of temptation, thoughts of another man's wife, thoughts of meaningless things, and thoughts of human burden. So, it was written in Deuteronomy by Moses our teacher, "They will be a sign and a proof against you and your offspring for all time. Because you would not serve the Eternal your God with joy and gladness over the abundance of everything. You will have to serve, in hunger and in thirst, naked and lacking everything." "In hunger." How so? When a person wishes to eat even barley bread, but has nothing, and then his enemies come and ask him for wheat bread and fatty meat. "In thirst." How so? When a person wishes he could drink just a drop of vinegar, or beer, but has nothing, and then his enemies come and ask him for the finest wine in the land. "Naked." How so? When a person wants to wear a wool or linen shirt, but has nothing, and then his enemies come and ask him for the finest silk in the land. "Lacking everything." Without a candle, without a knife, and without a table. Another interpretation of "lacking everything": Without vinegar

Avot D'Rabbi Natan - Chapter 20

and without salt. For this is a curse that people often given: May there is no vinegar or salt in your house!

He would also say: "Do not look at me, for I am blackened, scorched by the sun." These are all the Jewish girls who cast off the yolk of the Holy Blessed One, and accepted human kingship upon themselves.

The verse continues: "My mother's children were angry with me." This is Moses, who killed the Egyptian, as it says, "Sometime after that, when Moses had grown older, he went out among his brothers and saw what they were enduring…and he turned this way and that, and saw that there was no one there." What do we learn from "there was no one there"? This teaches that Moses brought the question before the council of angels who serve God, and asked them: Shall I kill this man? They said to him: Yes, kill him. And did Moses kill him with a sword? No, he killed him with words, as it says, "Are you saying you will kill me, just as you killed the Egyptian?" This teaches that Moses killed him by saying the Ineffable Name of God.

Another interpretation of "My mother's children are angry with me": this is Moses, who fled to Midian, as it says, "Pharaoh heard what happened, and sought to kill Moses, and Moses fled from Pharaoh. He arrived in the land of Midian, and sat down by a well…And some shepherds came and tried to drive Jethro's daughters away. And Moses got up and saved them, and gave water to their flocks." Then Moses came and sat among them to render judgment. He said: The general practice in the world is for men to fill the buckets and women to give water to the animals. Here, women draw the water and men give the water to the animals. There is a perversion of justice in this place! They are guilty by law, and have

Avot D'Rabbi Natan - Chapter 20

become guilty through this incident. Some say that the whole time Moses was standing near the mouth of the well, the water was bubbling up to meet him, and when he left, the water went back down. Then Moses said: Woe is me! For I have left my people and come to live among these heathens.

Another interpretation of "My mother's children are angry with me": This is Israel, who made the Golden Calf. At first, they said, "Everything the Eternal has said, we will do and we will understand." And then they went back and said, "These are your gods, Israel!"

Another interpretation of "My mother's children are angry with me": These are the spies, who slandered the land and caused Israel to die in the desert, as it says, "In this desert your carcasses will fall."

"They made me guard the vineyards". The Holy Blessed One said: Who is it that caused me to favor the heathens? Israel! For while the heathens live well, Israel are oppressed, scorned, and scattered about.

Another interpretation of "They made me guard the vineyards": This is Israel, who were exiled to Babylon. And prophets rose among them and told them to separate their donations and tithes. The people said to them: We were exiled because we did not separate our donations and tithes, and now you tell us we should separate them? And that is why it says, "They made me guard the vineyards."

Avot D'Rabbi Natan - Chapter 21

Chapter 21

Rabbi Dosa Ben Hyrcanus would say: Sleeping through the morning, drinking wine in the afternoon, the chatter of little children, and sitting around in the gathering houses with the common folk; these things drive a person from the world.

Sleeping through the morning, how so? This teaches that a person should not plan to sleep so late that the time for reciting the Shema will pass. As, if he does sleep that late, he will end up wasting time he could have spent studying Torah, as it says, "The door turns on its hinges, but the lazy one is still in his bed. The lazy one says: There is a leopard in my path. A lion roams the streets."

Drinking wine in the afternoon, how so? This teaches that a person should not plan to drink in the afternoon, because whenever he does, he ends up wasting all the time he could have spent studying Torah, as it says, "Woe is the land whose king is a child, and whose ministers eat late in the morning." And then, "Happy is the land whose king is a free man and whose ministers eat at the right time; with restraint, not guzzling." And what is the right time? One might say it is in some future yet to come, as it says, "I, the Eternal, will bring it about at the right time." Or, "At the right time Jacob will tell Israel what God has planned." The Holy Blessed One said to Bil'am, "At the right time," not: In the right time; that is, not in the time you live, but at some future time when I redeem Israel.

The chatter of little children, How so? This teaches that a person should not plan, when he is studying in his house, to chat with his wife and his sons and daughters. For when a person is studying in his house, and becomes distracted

Avot D'Rabbi Natan - Chapter 21

with his children and the people in his house, he ends up wasting time he could have spent studying Torah, as it says, "Do not let this book of Torah depart from your mouth; reflect on it day and night."

Sitting around in the gathering houses with the common folk, How so? This teaches that a person should not sit with those who sit around in the marketplace, or he will end up wasting time he could have spent studying Torah, as it says, "Happy is the man who does not walk in the counsel of the wicked …for only the Torah of the Eternal does he desire." Rabbi Meir said: What does it mean in the continuation of the verse by "sitting with those who mock"? Not to sit in the theaters of mockers in which they sentence people to death, as it says, "I hated the gathering of evildoers, and I will not sit with the wicked." And the evildoers are the wicked, as it says, "For the evildoers will be cut off." Where is their punishment? In the World to Come, as it says, "For behold, the day is coming that blazes like an oven, and all the sinister and all those who do wickedness will be like straw." These "sinister" ones are the mockers, as it says, "The sinister, arrogant one is called a mocker."

There is a story of Rabbi Akiva, who was sitting and teaching his students, when suddenly he remembered how he had spent his youth. He said: I give thanks before you, Lord my God, that you have placed my lot with those who sit in the study hall and not with those who sit around in the marketplace.

Avot D'Rabbi Natan - Chapter 22

Chapter 22

Rabbi Hanina Ben Dosa would say: Anyone whose fear of sin precedes his wisdom, his wisdom will endure, as it says, "The beginning of wisdom is fear of the Eternal." He would also say: Anyone whose actions are greater than his wisdom, his wisdom will endure, as it says, "We will do, and then we will understand."

They asked Rabban Yohanan Ben Zakkai: A wise person who fears sin – what is he like? He replied: Like a craftsman with his tool in hand. Then they asked: A wise person who does not fear sin – what is he like? He replied: Like a craftsman who does not have his tool in hand. Then they asked: A person who fears sin but is not wise – what is he like? He replied: Like someone who does not know the craft, but has a tool in his hand.

Rabbi Elazar Ben Azariah would say: If there is no Torah, there is no common decency. If there is no common decency, there is no Torah. He would also say: A person who has done good deeds, and has learned a lot of Torah – what is he like? Like a tree that stands near the water, whose branches are small, but whose roots are so strong that even if the four winds of the world all came and blew at it, it could not be moved from its place, as it says, "He is like a tree planted by streams of water." But a person who has not done good deeds and studies Torah, what is he like? Like a tree that stands in the desert, with small branches and small roots, and when a wind comes and blows at it, it uproots it and flips it over on its top, as it says, "You will be like a bush in the desert."

Rabban Gamliel would say: Make for yourself a teacher. Acquire for yourself a friend. A teacher for wisdom and

Avot D'Rabbi Natan - Chapter 22

a friend to study with. Remove yourself from all doubts, and do not get used to tithing by estimation.

His son Shimon would say: All my life, I grew up among the sages, and I never learned anything better for a person than silence. And if silence is good for the sages, how much more so for the foolish!

Wisdom does not produce words, and words do not produce wisdom; only action does. Anyone who talks too much bring about sin, as it says, "When there is too much talking, there is no lack of sin." And it says, "Even a fool, if he keeps silent, is deemed wise."

Avot D'Rabbi Natan - Chapter 23

Chapter 23

Ben Zoma would say: Who is wise? One who learns from every person, as it says, "From all my teachers I gained insight." Who is the humblest of all? One who is humble like Moses our teacher, as it says, "And the man Moses was exceedingly humble."

Who is the richest of all? One who is happy with what he has, as it says, "You will eat from the work of your hands, and you will be happy and prosperous." Who is the strongest of all? One who is able to conquer his desire, as it says, "Better to be forbearing than mighty, to have self-control than to conquer a city." And one who conquers his desire is considered as if he had conquered a city full of warriors, as it says, "One wise man prevailed over a city of warriors." The true warriors are warriors in Torah, as it says, "Mighty warriors do His bidding." Some say these are the angels who serve God, as it says, "Bless the Eternal, His angels, mighty warriors." And some say: One who can turn an enemy into his friend.

Rabbi Nehorai would say: Exile yourself to a place of Torah and do not say that it will come to you, or that your colleagues will do it for you. And do not rely on your own understanding. He would also say: Do not disparage any person and do not dismiss anything, as it says, "One who disparages a principle will become injured through it; one who respects a command will be rewarded."

He would also say: One, who studies Torah in his youth, what is he like? Like a calf which was tamed when it was still small, as it says, "Ephraim became a trained calf, but still wanted to thresh." One who studies Torah in his old age is like a cow that was never trained until it was too old, as it says, "Israel turned away like a stubborn cow."

Avot D'Rabbi Natan - Chapter 23

He would also say: One who studies Torah in his youth is like a woman who kneads dough when it is hot. One who studies Torah in his old age, what is he like? Like a woman who kneads dough when it is cold.

Rabbi Eliezer Ben Ya'akov would say: One who studies Torah in his youth is like letters written on fresh paper. One who studies Torah in his old age is like letters written on withered paper.

Rabban Shimon Ben Gamliel then added to what he said: One who studies Torah in his youth is like a young man who married a young woman. She was a good match for him, and he a good match for her. And she cast herself upon him, and he cast himself upon her. One who studies Torah in his old age, what is he like? Like an old man who married a young woman. She was a good match for him, but he was not a good match for her. She cast herself upon him, but he kept his distance from her, as it says, "Like arrows in the hand of a warrior are children of youth." And immediately afterward it says, "Happy is the man who fills his quiver with them." One who learns and then forgets is like a woman who gives birth to children and then buries them, as it says, "Even though they raise children, I will bereave people of them." Do not read "bereave" v'sikaltim, but rather, "cause them to forget" v'shikhahtim.

Rabbi Shimon Ben Elazar would say: One who studies Torah in his youth is like a doctor who is treating a wound, and has a scalpel to cut into it and medicine to heal it. One who studies Torah in his old age is like a doctor who is treating a wound, and has a scalpel to cut into it but no medicine to heal it. So, it is with words of Torah: they are marked in order for an individual to distinguish one from one another, and then arranged side

Avot D'Rabbi Natan - Chapter 23

by side, as it says, "Tie them to your fingers and write them on the tablet of your heart." And also, "Tie them to your heart always, and fasten them around your throat."

Avot D'Rabbi Natan - Chapter 24

Chapter 24

Elisha Ben Abuyah would say: A person who has done good deeds and has learned a lot of Torah, what is he like? Like a person who builds by placing stones down first and then setting bricks on top. Even if a flood comes, the building will stand firm and not be washed away from its place.

And a person who has not done good deeds but has learned Torah, what is he like? Like a person who builds by placing the bricks down first, and then placing stones on top. Even if a little water comes, it will topple the building right away.

He would also say: A person who has done good deeds and learned a lot of Torah, what is he like? Like bricks coated with plaster. Even if heavy rains fall on them, they will not move from their place. A person who has not done good deeds but has learned a lot of Torah is like bricks coated with plaster. Even if light rains fall on them, they crumble right away.

He would also say: A person who has done good deeds and has learned a lot of Torah is like a cup with a flat base. When one sets it down, even if it is knocked over, not all of its contents will spill. A person who has not done good deeds but has learned a lot of Torah is like a cup without a flat base. When one sets it down, it immediately falls over on its side, and all of its contents spill out.

He would also say: A person who has done good deeds and has learned a lot of Torah is like a horse that has fine equipment. A person who has not done good deeds but has learned a lot of Torah is like a horse without a bridle

Avot D'Rabbi Natan - Chapter 24

to restrain it. When a person wants to mount the horse, it throws him off in an instant.

He would also say: For one who studies Torah in his youth, the words of Torah are absorbed into his blood and come forth from his mouth with clear articulation. For one who studies Torah in his old age, the words of Torah are not absorbed into his blood and do not come forth from his mouth with clear articulation. And there is a well-known saying that: If you did not want them in your youth, you will not be able to get them in your old age.

He would also say: Words of Torah are as difficult to acquire as golden vessels. And they are as easy to lose as glass vessels, as it says, "It cannot be estimated by gold and glass." Gold is compared to glass to say that gold, when it is broken, can be fixed but glass vessels cannot be fixed when they are broken unless they are completely remade. And how can I understand the second half of the verse, "Nor exchanged for fine golden vessels"? This is to tell you that when one studies words of Torah and fulfills them; his face shines like fine gold. But when one studies words of Torah but does not fulfill them, his face is dark like glass.

He would also say: A person can study Torah for twenty years and forget it all in two years. How so? If he sat for six months and did not review what he had learned, he would begin to say that what was impure was pure, and what was pure was impure. After twelve months of no review, he would mix up the names of the sages. After eighteen months of no review, he would forget the beginnings of the tractates. After twenty-four months of no review, he would forget the beginnings of the chapters. Finally, he would have to sit and be silent. King Solomon said about such a person, "I passed by the field of a lazy

Avot D'Rabbi Natan - Chapter 24

man, and by the vineyard of a heartless person. It was all overgrown with thorns, its surface was covered with weeds, and the stone wall around it had been destroyed." And when the wall of a vineyard falls, soon enough the whole vineyard is destroyed.

He would also say: Anyone who helps his friend perform a mitzvah, the Torah considers it as if he had done it himself. A parable: To what can this be compared? It can be compared to a human king who captured a bird and gave it to one of his servants. The king said to him: Be careful with this bird, for if you treat it with care, all will be well. But if you do not, I will take your life for it. So did the Holy Blessed One say to Israel: If you observe these words of Torah that I have given to you, all will be well. But if not, I will take your lives because of them, as it says, "Just be very careful to protect your life, lest you forget these things that your eyes have seen.", "It is not an empty thing for you, for it is your very life."

Avot D'Rabbi Natan - Chapter 25

Chapter 25

Ben Azzai would say: When someone's mind is calm as a result of the wisdom, they have acquired that is a good sign. When someone's mind is not calm as a result of the wisdom they have acquired, that is a bad sign. When someone's mind is calm in the face of his desire, that is a good sign. When someone's mind is not calm in the face of his desire that is a bad sign. When the sages look kindly upon someone at the time of his death, that is a good sign. When the sages do not look kindly upon someone, that is a bad sign. When someone is facing upward at the time of his death, that is a good sign. When someone is facing downward, that is a bad sign. When someone looks people in the eye, that is a good sign. When someone avoids looking people in the eye, that is a bad sign. When someone's face shines, that is a good sign. When someone's face is gloomy, that is a bad sign.

At the hour of Rabban Yohanan Ben Zakkai's death, he raised his voice and cried. His students said to him: Rabbi! You are a tall pillar, a light to the world, a mighty hammer; so why do you cry? He said to them: Am I going to face a human king? If he were angry with me, it would be only in this world. And if he imprisoned me or killed me, it would be only in this world. And what's more, I would be able to pacify him with words, or bribe him with money. But no, I am going to face the King of all kings, the Holy Blessed One. And if He is angry with me, it will be in this world and in the World to Come. And what's more, I cannot pacify Him with words or bribe Him with money. So, I have two paths before me: one that leads to Paradise, and one that leads to Gehenna, and I do not know if He will force me into Gehenna or bring me into

Avot D'Rabbi Natan - Chapter 25

Paradise. For the verse says about Him: "All who go down into the dirt will submit before him." With regard to Moses, it says that he breathed his last breath and died, and was gathered to his people. It also says, "I will remove my hand." And then it says, "And He spread it out before me, and it had writing on the front and on the back." "On the front" refers to this world; "on the back" refers to the World to Come. Another interpretation: "On the front" refers to the sufferings of the righteous in this world and the tranquility of the wicked in this world. "On the back" refers to the reward for the righteous in the Future to Come, and the punishment for the wicked in Gehenna.

The verse from Ezekiel continues: "And on it were written lamentations, dirges, and woes". "Lamentations" refers to the punishment of the wicked in this world, as it says, "This is the lamentation with which they shall lament for her; the women of the nations shall lament for her." "Dirges" refers to the reward for the righteous in the Time to Come, as it says, "Upon the ten-stringed instrument, and upon the lyre and the dirge of the harp." "Woe" refers to the punishment of the wicked in the World to Come, as it says, "Woe will come upon woe, rumor upon rumor."

He would also say: Clear your house of impurity, and prepare a chair for Hezekiah, king of Judah.

He would also say: If someone dies with a clear mind, that is a good sign; with a confused mind, a bad sign. If someone dies while speaking, that is a good sign; in silence, a bad sign. If someone dies while speaking words of Torah, that is a good sign; while speaking trivial words, a bad sign. If someone dies in happiness, that is a good sign; in sadness, a bad sign. If someone dies while

Avot D'Rabbi Natan - Chapter 25

laughing, that is a good sign; while crying, a bad sign. If someone dies just before the Sabbath, that is a good sign; just after the Sabbath, a bad sign. If someone dies just before Yom Kippur that is a bad sign; just after Yom Kippur, a good sign.

When Rabbi Eliezer became sick, they say it was the eve of the Sabbath. Rabbi Akiva and his companions came in to visit him. He was sleeping in his room, so they sat in the entrance hall. His son Hyrcanus went in to take off his father's tefillin, but his father would not let him, and began to cry. Hycanus came out and said to the sages: My masters, it seems to me that my father is confused. But his father called out: My son, I am not confused – you are confused! For you have not lit the Sabbath candles, for which you can be sentenced to death by divine decree. But I was just wearing tefillin, which is forbidden to be worn on the Sabbath only by rabbinic practice. When the sages saw that he was of clear mind they went in and sat before him, at a distance of four cubits. They said to him: Rabbi, a circular cushion, a ball, a mannequin, an amulet, and a torn prayer box – what is their status with regard to whether they can become impure? He said to them: They can become impure, and you should immerse them in water just as they are. Be very careful to do this, because these are important laws that were said to Moses on Mount Sinai. So, they continued asking about ritual purity and impurity, and immersions. They would say: Rabbi, what about this? And he would say: Impure. What about that? And he would say: Pure. In this way he answered all their questions about what was pure and what was impure.

Afterward, Rabbi Eilezer said to the sages: I wonder if the students of this generation will be punished by death

Avot D'Rabbi Natan - Chapter 25

at the hands of Heaven. They replied: Rabbi, why? He said to them: Because they have not come and apprenticed with me.

Then he said to Akiva Ben Yosef: Akiva, why did you not come to apprentice with me? Rabbi Akiva said: I did not have any time to come. He replied: I wonder if you will die a natural death.

Some say they never said any of this; rather, when Rabbi Eliezer first said this about the students, Akiva's blood started racing inside of him, and he said: And Rabbi, how will I die? And Rabbi Eliezer said: Rabbi Akiva, your death will be the worst of all. Then Rabbi Akiva went and sat before him and said: Rabbi, teach me. Rabbi Eliezer began by teaching him three hundred laws about impure white patches of skin baheret. Then Rabbi Eliezer raised both of his arms and laid them on his chest, and said: Oy, these two arms of mine are like two Torah scrolls that will vanish from the world! For if all the seas were ink, and all the reeds were quills, and every person was a scribe, they still could not write down everything that I have read and taught. I apprenticed with the sages in the academy and did not forget a thing I witnessed, not even a drop out of the sea. I never ceased learning except to dip my quill into ink. I could teach three hundred laws just on the verse, "Do not let a witch live" – and some say it was three thousand laws! – But no one ever asked me about them except for Akiva Ben Yosef, who once said, Rabbi, teach me how they plant squash through witchcraft, and how we uproot them. And I answered, with one word; the whole field is filled with squash. So, he said to me, Rabbi, you have taught me about how they are planted; now teach me about how they are uprooted. And I said, with one word, they can all be gathered together into one place.

Avot D'Rabbi Natan - Chapter 25

Rabbi Elazar Ben Azariah said to him: Rabbi, what about a sandal on a mannequin's leg? He answered: Pure. In this way he kept answering questions about what was pure and what was impure, until his soul departed in a state of purity. Immediately, Rabbi Elazar Ben Azariah tore his clothes and wept. Then he went out and said the sages: My Masters, come and see Rabbi Eliezer, who will be pure in the World to Come because his soul left in a state of purity.

After the Sabbath, Rabbi Akiva came and found Rabbi Eliezer being taken in a coffin from Caesarea to Lod. Immediately, he tore his clothes and pulled at his hair until blood began to come out and drip onto the ground. And he screamed and cried and said: Woe is me, my master, for I have lost you! Woe is me, my master, for I have lost you! My master, you have left this whole generation like an orphan! At the head of his funeral line, he said, "My father, my father, the chariot of Israel and all its horsemen!" You have left money for me, and I have no table [i.e. money changer] to exchange them.

Ben Azzai would say: Run to fulfill even a minor mitzvah.

He would also say: If you have performed only one mitzvah without regrets, it will bring you to performing many more mitzvot. But one who commits even one transgression without regrets, it will bring him to make other transgressions. For one mitzvah leads to another and one transgression leads to another. For the reward for a mitzvah is another commandment and the punishment for a transgression is another transgression.

He would also say: Stop yourself from transgressing, so that you are rewarded for your effort. Do not wait for others to stop you, for then they will receive the reward.

Avot D'Rabbi Natan - Chapter 25

He would also say: Take yourself down two or three levels, and then come back. For better that they say to you: Step up! Rather than: Step down!" as it says, "For it is better to be told: Ascend! Than to be degraded in front of nobility."

Three kinds of life are not worth living. And they are: one who has to find food at his friend's table, one who lives in an attic, and one whose wife has control over him. And some say also: One whose suffering has control over his body.

He would also say: It is easier to rule over the whole world than to sit and teach before people wrapped in sheets, meaning their inner character is nothing like their outer appearance.

Avot D'Rabbi Natan - Chapter 26

Chapter 26

Rabbi Akiva would say: A sense of humor is a fence for honor. Silence is a fence for wisdom. Abstinence is a fence for vows. Holiness is a fence for purity. Fear of sin is a fence for humility.

He would also say: Do not hang around with cynics, for you may begin to learn from their ways. Do not break bread with an unlearned priest, for you may end up desecrating holy things. Do not break your vows; for you may come to break your oaths. Do not accustom yourself to eating big meals, for you may end up having to eat scraps. Do not cause yourself to doubt, for you may then cause yourself to be overconfident. Do not leave the Land of Israel, for you may end up worshiping idols, just as David said, "For they have driven me out today, so that I cannot have a share in the Eternal's inheritance, but am told to go and serve other gods." Do you actually think King David would worship idols? Rather, David was saying that anyone who leaves the Land of Israel and goes to a foreign country, it is as if he were worshiping idols.

He would also say: Anyone who is buried in any foreign country, it is as if he were buried in Babylon. Anyone who is buried in Babylon, it is as if he were buried in the Land of Israel. Anyone who is buried in the Land of Israel, it is as if he were buried underneath the altar, for all of the Land of Israel is fit for the altar. Anyone who is buried underneath the altar, it is as if he were buried under the Throne of Glory, as it says, "A Throne of Glory, exalted from the beginning, is the place of our Sanctuary."

He would also say: An unlearned person cannot be truly pious. A timid person cannot learn, nor can an impatient

Avot D'Rabbi Natan - Chapter 26

person teach.

He would also say: Why do Torah scholars die young? Not because they commit adultery, and not because they steal, but because they interrupt their Torah learning with casual conversation. And then they do not come back to the place where they left off.

Rabbi Shimon Ben Elazar would say: When the people of Israel are in foreign lands, they worship idolatry without meaning to. How so? A Samaritan makes a party for his son. He sends out an invitation to all the Jews in his city. Even though they eat and drink their own food, and bring their own attendants who stand and pour for them, it is still considered as if they ate from the sacrifices of the dead, as it says, "They will call to you, and you will eat their sacrifices."

Rabbi Eliezer HaModa'i would say: Anyone who violates the Sabbath, scorns the festivals, disregards circumcision, or attempts to reveal the flaws of the Torah, even though he may be learned in Torah and have done many good deeds, he has no share in the World to Come.

Rabbi Akiva would say: Anyone who marries a woman who is not proper for him, transgresses five commandments: "Do not take vengeance", "Do not bear a grudge", "Do not hate your brother in your heart", "Love your fellow as yourself", and "Let your brother live with you". Because he will hate her he will want her to die, and this will cause fewer children to be born into the world.

He would also say: Anyone who eats food that is not good for the body, upon which he does not make a blessing transgresses three commandments: He disgraces himself, he disgraces the food, and he makes a blessing on something that is not for his betterment.

Avot D'Rabbi Natan - Chapter 26

Rabbi Yehudah Ben Ilai would say: When a person who dies and leaves behind a son who never learned Torah from his father, and then that son goes and studies Torah from others, this child will always be seeking approval.

Rabbi Eliezer HaKappar would say: Do not be like the upper part of the doorway, which no person hand can reaches. And do not be like the upper beam, which displays engraved images, nor like the middle beam, which knocks into the legs. Rather, be like the threshold, which everyone steps on, and which will remain standing even when the rest of the building has been destroyed.

Avot D'Rabbi Natan - Chapter 27

Chapter 27

Rabbi Yosei would say: Anyone who honors the Torah will be honored by others, as it says, "For those that honor Me, I will honor; and those who scorn me will not be taken seriously." "Those who honor Me, I will honor" – this refers to Pharaoh, king of Egypt, who showed honor to the One who spoke and brought the world into being when he marched out at the head of his troops. His servants said to him: The custom is that king's march out only at the rear of their troops, and you are marching out at the head of your troops. He said to them: Am I going out to encounter a human king? No, I am going to encounter the King of all kings, the Holy Blessed One. That is why the Holy Blessed One showed honor to him by punishing him personally, as it says, "I have likened you, my darling, to a mare in Pharaoh's chariots."

Rabbi Papius would say: The congregation of Israel was favored above the horses in Pharaoh's chariot, as it says, "You led your horses into the sea."

Rabbi Yehoshua Ben Karha would say: When Pharaoh went into the sea; he rode on a male horse. But then the Holy Blessed One revealed it to be a female horse, as it says, "To a mare in Pharaoh's chariots." But was it perhaps not a chariot, but a cherub? As it says, "He mounted a cherub and flew, gliding on the wings of the wind." What happened is that the cherub appeared like a team of female horses, and they all went into the sea.

Those who scorn me will not be taken seriously" – this is Sennacherib, who scorned the One who spoke and brought the world into being, thus scorning the Holy Blessed One, as it says, "Through your servants you have blasphemed my Lord. Because you said: Thanks to my

Avot D'Rabbi Natan - Chapter 27

vast charity, I have climbed the highest mountains to the remotest parts of the Lebanon, and have cut down its loftiest cedars, its choicest cypresses, and have reached its highest peak, its densest forest. I have drawn and drunk water. I have dried up all the streams of Egypt with the soles of my feet." Therefore, the Holy Blessed One punished him through an emissary, who shaved his head and beard, and sent him back in shame to his own land.

Rabbi Yishmael the son of Rabbi Yohanan Ben Beroka would say: One who learns in order to teach, etc. He would also say: You need not be ready to study the entire Torah, but neither are you free to leave it all aside. Rather, one who continues to add to his learning adds greatly to his reward.

Rabbi Elazar Ben Hamsa would say: The study of bird offerings and the calculations of menstruation – these are the essence of the Law.

Rabbi Yohanan Ben Nuri would say: Legal matters, ritual purity, bird offerings, and the calculations of menstruation – these are the essence of the Torah.

He would also say: Setting the great table, and establishing and supporting a court – both bring goodness into to the world.

Rabbi Yohanan Ben Dahabai would say: Anyone who says, this law is unreasonable, has no share in the World to Come.

He would also say: Do not keep away from a measurement without boundaries, or from work without end. A parable: To what can this be compared? It can be compared to someone who is supposed to take water from the sea and put it on dry land. The sea gets no smaller and the land is not filled up with water. So, he becomes frustrated. Say to such a person, Empty one! Why are

Avot D'Rabbi Natan - Chapter 27

you so frustrated? Every day you are paid a golden dinar! Rabbi Eliezer Ben Shamua would say: Let your student's honor be dearer to you than your own. Honor your friend with the reverence you have for your teacher. And revere your teacher with the reverence you have for Heaven. This teaches that one's student's honor should be as important to him as his friend's honor. Everyone should learn from Moses our teacher, who said to Joshua, "Choose men for us." He did not say: Choose for me, but "choose for us." This teaches that Moses treated Joshua like an equal, even though Moses was the master and Joshua was his student. Where do we learn that your friend's honor should be as dear to you as your teacher's? From what it says, "Then Aaron said to Moses: Oh, my lord." But wasn't Moses his younger brother? Yet this shows that he treated him like a teacher. And from where do we know that your teacher's honor should be as dear to you as the honor of Heaven? From what it says, "And Joshua, who was Moses' attendant from the time he was young, answered and said: My Lord, Moses, stop them!" For he regarded Moses as equivalent to the Divine Presence itself.

At first, they would say: there is grain in Judah, straw in the Galilee, and chaff on the other side of the Jordan. But then they began to say: There is no grain in Judah. There is no straw in the Galilee, but there is chaff. And on the other side of the Jordan, there is neither.

Avot D'Rabbi Natan - Chapter 28

Chapter 28

Rabbi Natan would say: There is no love like the love of Torah. There is no wisdom like the wisdom of the "way of the world." There is no beauty like the beauty of Jerusalem. There are no riches like the riches of Media. There is no power like the power of Persia. There is no promiscuity like the promiscuity of Arabs. There is no arrogance like the arrogance of Elam. There is no flattery like the flattery of Babylon, as it says, "And he said to me, to build a house for it in the land of Shinar." And there is no witchcraft like the witchcraft of Egypt.

Rabbi Shimon Ben Elazar would say: When a sage life in the Land of Israel and then leaves, his wisdom is impaired. Whereas one who lives there is praised, and even if he is impaired, he is still praised above any sages who live in foreign lands. They give a parable to explain what this can be compared to: When steel from Nadoi is imported across the sea, even if it diminishes in quality, it is still much better than any of the best metal in those countries, it is imported to.

Rabbi Shimon Ben Gamliel would say: Anyone who brings peace into his own home is regarded by the Torah as if he had brought peace to everyone in Israel. And anyone who brings jealousy and competitiveness into his own home is regarded by the Torah as if he had brought jealousy and competition to Israel. For everyone is a king in his own home, as it says, "So that every man shall rule over his own home."

Rabban Gamliel would say: The Cuthean Kingdom survives off of four things: taxes, bathhouses, theaters, and tithes.

He would also say: Words of Torah are as difficult to

Avot D'Rabbi Natan - Chapter 28

acquire as wool garments, and as easy to lose as linen garments. Words of foolishness and nonsense are as easy to acquire and as difficult to lose as sackcloth. Sometimes a person buys sackcloth in the marketplace for a sela, and then uses it for four or five years. Rabbi Yehudah HaNasi would say: Anyone who indulges in the pleasures of this world prevents himself from experiencing the pleasures of the World to Come. And anyone who denies himself the pleasure of this world is given all the pleasures of the World to Come.

He would also say: Righteous people who suffer in this world – to what can they be compared? They can be compared to a chef who prepares a meal for himself. Even though he has gone to all the trouble, in the end he will be able to eat and others will not. But wicked people who suffer in this world – to what can they be compared? They can be compared to a chef who has prepared a meal for others. Even though he has gone to all the trouble, in the end it is others who will eat and not the chef.

He would also say: Let your secrets be revealed. But do not say to your friend that which should not be heard.

Hillel would say: Do not separate yourself from the community.

He would also say: The more one eats, the more one excretes. The more meat, the more worms and maggots there are. The more good deeds one does, the more peace one feels inside.

Rabbi Elazar Ben Shamua would say: There are three types of Torah scholars – the Hewn Stone, the Corner Stone, and the Polished Stone. The Hewn Stone – what is he like? This is a scholar who studies Midrash. When another scholar comes to him and asks him a question about the Midrash, he is able to answer. He is like a hewn

Avot D'Rabbi Natan - Chapter 28

stone, which has only one surface. The Corner Stone – what is he like? This is a scholar who studies Midrash and Halakhah. When one scholar comes and asks him a question about Midrash, he is able to answer. And when another scholar asks about Halakhah, he is able to answer. He is like a corner stone, which has only two surfaces. The Polished Stone – what is he like? This is a scholar who studies Midrash, Halakhah, Aggadah, and Tosefta. When one scholar comes and asks about Midrash, he is able to answer. And when another scholar asks about Halakhah, he is able to answer. And when another scholar asks about Tosefta, he is able to answer. And when another scholar asks about Aggadah, he is able to answer. He is like a polished stone, which has four surfaces, one on each of its four sides.

Rabbi Yehudah Ben Ilai would say: Anyone who makes words of Torah primary and the way of the world secondary will be made primary in this world. Anyone who makes the way of the world primary and words of Torah secondary will be made secondary in this world. They give a parable to explain what this can be compared to: It can be compared to a troop has to pass between two paths, one of fire and one of snow. If it goes too near the fire, it will be burned. If it goes too near the snow, it will be frozen. What should it do? It must go between them, and be careful not to be burned by the fire or frozen by the snow.

Rabbi Shimon ben Elazar said: "Do not try to appease your friend during his hour of anger; Nor comfort him at the hour while his dead still lies before him; Nor question him at the hour of his vow; Nor strive to see him in the hour of his disgrace".

Avot D'Rabbi Natan - Chapter 29

Chapter 29

Rabbi Shimon Ben Elazar would say in the name of Rabbi Meir: Do not try to make your friend feel better when he is still angry. And do not attempt to comfort him when he is still in mourning. And do not ask him if he wants something when he has taken a vow not to have it. And do not come to his house to try to see him on the day of his festival. And some say: If you have friends, some of whom challenge you and some of whom praise you, love the ones who challenge you and hate the ones who praise you. For those who challenge you are bringing you into the World to Come, and those who praise you are taking you out of the world.

He would also say: Anywhere a person goes, his heart goes. Where he stays, his heart stays. When he is settled, those around him feel settled.

He would also say: Anyone who commits himself to studying words of Torah becomes surrounded by a circle of committed colleagues. And anyone who neglects studying words of Torah becomes surrounded by a circle of neglectful companions. And then he is attacked by a lion, a wolf, a tiger, a hyena, or a snake. Or soldiers or thieves come and surround him and take his money, as it says, "For there is a God who judges upon the earth."

Shaul Ben Nanas came and said: There are four types of Torah scholars. You have one who teaches himself but does not teach others, one who teaches others but does not teach himself, one who teaches himself and others, and one who teaches neither himself nor others.

The one who teaches himself but does not teach others – what is he like? He studies a chapter, or two or three, but he does not teach them to anyone else. He reviews them,

Avot D'Rabbi Natan - Chapter 29

and makes sure he does not forget them. This is the one who teaches himself but does not teach others.

The one who teaches others but does not teach himself – what is he like? He studies a whole section, or two or three, and then he teaches them to others. But he does not review them himself, and he forgets them. This is the one who teaches others but not himself.

The one who teaches himself and others – what is he like? He learns a whole section, to two or three, and then he teaches them to others. Then he reviews them, making sure he does not forget them, until he has them completely mastered. This is the one who teaches himself and others.

The one who teaches neither himself nor others – what is he like? He studies a whole section, or two or three. But he does not teach them to others, and does not review them himself, and eventually he forgets them. This is the one who teaches neither himself nor others.

Rabbi Hananya Ben Ya'akov would say: When someone is up late at night learning words of Torah, this is a good sign. When someone is up late at night chatting, this is a bad sign.

Rabbi Ya'akov Ben Hananya would say: When someone stays up late at night, and never speaks a word of Torah, it would be good and proper if his mother's umbilical cord had been pulled back and he had never come out into the air and seen this world.

Rabbi Elazar HaKappar would say: Anyone who respects his friends only for their money, in the end will be sent away from them in disgrace. And anyone who disgraces his friends in order to fulfill a mitzvah, in the end will be sent away from them honorably.

How do we know that anyone who respects his friends?

Avot D'Rabbi Natan - Chapter 29

only for their money, in the end will be sent away from them in disgrace? For this is what we find with Bil'am the wicked, who respected Balak for his money, as it says, "And Bil'am answered, saying to Balak's servants: If Balak gives me his house full of silver and gold." And how do we know he was sent away in disgrace? For it says, "Now, get out of here and go back to your own place…for the Eternal has denied you honor."

And how do we know that anyone who disgraces his friends in order to fulfill a mitzvah, in the end will be sent away from them honorably? For this is what we find with Moses our teacher, who disgraces Pharaoh in order to fulfill a mitzvah, as it says, "All of your servants shall come down and bow before me, saying." Now, was Pharaoh up on a roof and was Moses down on the ground? No, what Moses meant was: Even if all your servants who stand up and bow before you on your platform were to get up and beg me, I would not listen to them. And how do we know he was sent away honorably? For it says, "On the day after the Passover offering, the Israelites went out with a raised hand."

Rabbi Matya Ben Heresh went to Rabbi Yishmael Ben Elazar HaKappar in Ludkia in order to learn about the four categories of atonement. He said to him: Have you heard about the four categories of atonement that Rabbi Yishmael used to teach? He replied: I have heard of three, and that repentance is essential for each one. One verse says, "Return, you wayward children, says the Eternal, and I will heal your afflictions." And another verse says, "On that day, he will atone for you, to purify you." And another verse says, "I will attend to their transgressions with my staff, and to their sins with plagues." And another verse says, "This sin will not be forgiven until

Avot D'Rabbi Natan - Chapter 29

you die." How do we make sense of all these? If a person transgresses a positive commandment and then repents, he is forgiven immediately. This is what is meant by "Return, you wayward children." If a person transgresses a negative commandment and repents, the repentance is held over until Yom Kippur atones for him, as it says, "On that day, he will atone for you." If a person transgresses a commandment for which he incurs spiritual excommunication karet or death by the court, and then repents, the repentance and Yom Kippur are held over until he is cleansed through suffering. This is what is meant by "I will attend to their transgressions with my staff." But someone who profanes the heavenly Name has no possibility of repenting and waiting for forgiveness. Suffering will not cleanse him. Yom Kippur will not atone for him. They are all held over until death comes and cleanses him. This is what is meant by "This sin will not be forgiven until you die."

Isi Ben Yehudah would say: Why do great Torah scholars die before their time? Not because they commit adultery, and not because they steal. Rather, it is because they disgrace themselves.

Rabbi Yitzchak Ben Pinchas would say: Anyone who has studied Midrash but has not studied Halakhah has never really tasted wisdom. Anyone who has studied Halakhah but has not studied Midrash has never really tasted the fear of sin.

He would also say: Anyone who has studied Midrash but has not studied Halakhah is like a strong person who is unarmed. Anyone who has studied Halakhah but has not studied Midrash is like a weak person with a weapon in his hand. Anyone who has studied both is like a person who is both strong and armed.

Avot D'Rabbi Natan - Chapter 29
He would also say: Be careful when greeting other people. Do not get in the middle of a conflict, and do not try to see it. Return to a place of friends. And be a tail to lions rather than a head to foxes.

Avot D'Rabbi Natan - Chapter 30

Chapter 30

Rabbi Natan Ben Yosef would say: Anyone who neglects words of Torah because of his wealth will come to neglect them because of poverty. And anyone who fulfills words of Torah in poverty will come to fulfill them in wealth.

He would also say: Comforting mourners, visiting the sick and acts of kindness bring good to the world.

Rabbi Meir would say: When someone commits a transgression out of uncertainty, the Torah considers it as if he had done it out of certainty. How so? If a person sins, and becomes aware of his sin, he must bring a sin offering worth one sela or a tenth of a bushel of grain worth one dupondium. But if he is uncertain about whether or not he sinned, he must bring a guilt offering worth two sela. For which is the greater force, reward or punishment? Surely one must say reward. Therefore, we can make an a fortiori inference: If punishment is the weaker force, and one who commits a transgression out of uncertainty will be considered to have done it out of certainty, then all the more so will a reward be given even when it is uncertain whether he deserves it.

Rabbi Natan Ben Yosef would say: When someone commits a transgression accidentally, the Torah considers it as if he had done it on purpose. How so? When someone commits involuntary manslaughter, he is exiled to a city of refuge. But if someone finds him before he reaches the city and kills him to avenge the first death, the avenger is not held culpable. But if someone murders intentionally, and someone comes to avenge the death and kills the murderer, then he is exiled because of it. For which is the greater force, reward or punishment? Surely one must say reward. So, if punishment is the weaker

Avot D'Rabbi Natan - Chapter 30

force, then when someone commits a transgression accidentally and the Torah considers it as if he had done it on purpose, then all the more so would one be rewarded even when he has done a good deed accidentally.

Rabbi Akiva would say: Anyone who associates with sinners, even if he does not do as they do, receives punishment just as they do. How so? Two people testify against a third person and say: This person killed someone. If they are then discovered to have lied, they will be sentenced to death. And if, when they are taken out to be stoned, another person runs up after them and comes forward and says: I know something else about them, they tell him to give testimony. If he too is discovered to have lied, then he too is sentenced to death. When they take him out to be stoned, he will say: Woe is me, for if I had never come forward, I would not have been sentenced to death! Now that I have accused them, I too will die. They say to him, "Empty one! Even if one hundred people came after you, and then were discovered to have lied, they all would have been killed. For which is the greater force, reward or punishment? Surely one must say reward. So, if punishment is the weaker force, and someone who associates with sinners – even if he does not do as they do – receives punishment, then all the more so would one be rewarded if he associated with those who do good deeds.

Rabbi Shimon would say: Such is the punishment for a liar, that even when he speaks the truth, no one listens to him. So, we find with the children of Jacob, who deceived their father. In the beginning he believed them, as it says, "They took Joseph's coat, slaughtered a goat," and then it says, "He recognized it, and said: This is my son's coat! But afterward, even when they spoke the truth to him, he

Avot D'Rabbi Natan - Chapter 30

did not believe them, as it says, "His heart became numb, for he did not believe them." "They told him, and said: Joseph is still alive… But he did not believe them."

Some say that the Holy Spirit that had departed from Jacob now returned to him, as it says, "And the spirit of their father Jacob was revived."

Avot D'Rabbi Natan - Chapter 31

Chapter 31

Rabbi Ahai Ben Yoshaya would say: To what can someone who buys produce from the marketplace be compared? He can be compared to an infant whose mother has died, and is taken to be nursed by other mothers, but is never fully satisfied. To what can someone who buys bread from the marketplace be compared? He can be compared to one who has had a grave dug for him and been buried. One who eats from his own farm is like an infant who is nurtured by his own mother's breast.

He would also say: When a person eats from his own farm, his mind is calm. And even when a person eats food from his father's or mother's farm, or from his children's farm, his mind is not calm – not to mention when he eats food from a stranger's farm.

The world was created with ten utterances. Why were all ten necessary? In order to teach you that anyone who performs one commandment, or keeps one Sabbath, or saves one life, the Torah considers it as if he had sustained the entire world, which was created with ten utterances. And anyone who commits one transgression, or breaks one Sabbath, or causes one life to be lost, the Torah considers it as if he had destroyed the entire world, which was created with ten utterances. For this is what we find with Cain, who killed his brother Abel, as it says, "The voice of your brother's bloods cries out to me from the ground." It should say "blood," but it says "bloods." This teaches that it was also the blood of his children and his children's children, and all his future generations, until the end of the human line that would have one day descended from him. They all stood up and cried out

Avot D'Rabbi Natan - Chapter 31

before the Holy Blessed One. So, you learn from this that one person is considered as important as the entire work of Creation.

Rabbi Nehemiah would say: Where do we learn that one person is considered as important as the entire work of Creation? Because it says, "This is the book of the generations of humanity," and prior to that it said, "These are the generations of the heavens and the earth when they were created." Just as previously there was creating and making, so too here there is creating and making. This teaches that the Holy Blessed One showed Adam all the generations that would come from him, as if they rose up and played before him. And some say that he was shown only his righteous descendants, as it says, "All who were inscribed for life in Jerusalem."

Rabbi Yehoshua Ben Karha would say: See, it says, "Your eyes see my unformed substance, they were all recorded in your book." This teaches that the Holy Blessed One showed Adam the first person every generation and its preachers, community servants, leaders, prophets, warriors, sinners, and saints, and said to him, "In this generation this one will be a king. In that generation this one will be a scholar."

Rabbi Eliezer the son of Rabbi Yosei HaGalili would say: Nine hundred and seventy-four generations before the world was created, the Torah was written and placed on the bosom of the Holy Blessed One, and it sang a song with the angels who serve God, as it says, "I was raised with Him, a source of delight to Him every day…rejoicing before Him on the face of His earth." They gave a parable: To what can this be compared? It can be compared to someone who took a piece of wood and wanted to carve lots of figures into it. But there was

Avot D'Rabbi Natan - Chapter 31

not enough room on the wood, and so he was sad. But then he began drawing pictures on the ground, and kept walking and drew many, many pictures. So, too, the Holy Blessed One – may His great name be blessed forever and ever – in His wisdom and insight, created the whole world, with the heavens and the earth, above and below. And He fashioned within the human being everything that He created in His world. He created forests in the world, and He created forests on human beings – that is, their hair. He created evil beasts in the world, and He created evil beasts in human beings – that is, the intestines of a person. He created thorns in the world, and He created thorns on human beings – that is, their ears. He created scent in the world, and He created scent in human beings – that is, in their noses. He created a sun in the world, and He created a sun in human beings – that is, a person's light. Putrid waters in the world and putrid waters in human beings – that is the water that drips from their noses. Salty waters in the world and salty waters in human beings – that is, the tears in their eyes. Rivers in the world and rivers in human beings – that is, their tears. Walls in the world, and walls in human beings – that is, a person's lips. Doors in the world and doors in human beings – that is, a person's teeth. Skies in the world and skies in human beings – that is, a person's tongue. Sweet waters in the world, and sweet waters in human beings – that is, a person's spit. Chiseled stones in the world and chiseled stones in human beings – that is, a person's jaws. Towers in the world, and towers in human beings – that is, a person's neck. Sail-yards in the world, and sail-yards on human beings – that is, a person's arms. Spikes in the world, and spikes on human beings – that is, a person's fingers. A king in the world and a king in the human being

Avot D'Rabbi Natan - Chapter 31

– that is, his head. Clusters in the world, and clusters in human beings – that is, in their blood. Advisers in the world and advisers in human beings – that is, their kidneys. Millstones in the world and millstones in human beings – that is, their stomachs. Grinding mills in the world, and grinding mills in human beings – that is, their spleens. Garbage heaps in the world, and garbage heaps in human beings – that is, a person's bowels. Pits in the world, and pits in human beings – that is, a person's navel. Running waters in the world, and running waters in human beings – that is, a person's urine. Life in the world, and life in human beings – that is, a person's blood. Trees in the world, and trees in human beings – that is, a person's bones. Hills in the world, and hills on human beings – that is, a person's buttocks. Mortars and pestles in the world, and mortars and pestles in human beings – that is, their knees and knee-sockets. Horses in the world, and horses in human beings – that is, a person's thighs. An angel of death in the world, and an angel of death in human beings – that is, a person's heels. Mountains and valleys in the world, and mountains and valleys in human beings – when they stand, they are like a mountain, and when they fall, they are like a valley. Now you have seen that everything the Holy Blessed One created in His world, He created also in human beings.

Avot D'Rabbi Natan - Chapter 32

Chapter 32

There were ten generations from Adam until Noah.

And why was it necessary to bring all those people into the world? This teaches you that even as all those generations continued to anger the Holy Blessed One, He did not bring the flood upon them because of the righteous and saintly among them. And some say that as long as Methuselah was alive, the flood did not come upon the world; and even when Methuselah died, it was still held off for another seven days, as it says, "And it was seven days, and the waters of the flood were on the earth." What was happening during those seven days? These were the seven days of mourning for that righteous man, who had prevented the punishment. That is why it says, "And it was seven days."

Another interpretation of, "And it was seven days": This teaches that the Holy Blessed One fixed a specific time, after 120 years, hoping that they might repent. But they did not, and so it says, "And it was seven days" [i.e., the final seven days of the countdown].

Another interpretation of, "And it was seven days": This teaches that the Holy Blessed One changed the order of the world which was created in seven days for them, and had the sun rise from the west and set in the east, hoping that maybe they would understand and become afraid and repent. But they did not, and so it says, "And it was seven days."

Another interpretation: This teaches that the Holy Blessed One set a table for them, and gave them a taste of the World to Come, so that they would gather together and say to one another, "Oy, for we have lost all this goodness, and we have caused the destruction of our

Avot D'Rabbi Natan - Chapter 32

descendants from the earth, as it says, "And God saw the earth, and it had been destroyed."

Rabbi Elazar Ben Parta would say about the verse, "My spirit shall not judge human beings forever," that the Holy Blessed one said: I will not judge them until I double their reward, as it says, "They spend their days well and their years pleasantly, and they calmly go down into Sheol." Rabbi Yosei HaGalili would say: See, it says, "My spirit shall not judge"; the Holy Blessed One said: I do not equate those with evil intentions to those with good intentions. Until when? Until their final judgment has been sealed. But when it is sealed, then both are judged equally for their sins.

He would also say: The righteous have their desire for evil taken away and are given a desire for good, as it says, "My heart has been hollowed out inside of me." The wicked have their desire for good taken away and are given a desire for evil, as it says, "Sin speaks to the wicked in his heart. There is no fear of God in his sight." Those who are not entirely righteous or entirely wicked beinomim are given both, and those who move toward their evil desires are judged by them, while those who move toward their good desires are judged by them, as it says, "For he who stands at the right of the needy, to save him from those who judge his soul."

Rabbi Shimon Ben Elazar would say: See, it says, "My spirit shall not judge," for the Holy Blessed One said: I will not judge the wicked until I pay the righteous their reward. How long will this last? During the time of the wicked in this world. But in the World to Come, the verse says, "His spirit leaves him, and he returns to the ground." Rabbi Akiva would say: See, it says, "My spirit shall not judge human beings forever," for the Holy Blessed One

Avot D'Rabbi Natan - Chapter 32

said: they cannot judge themselves, for they are just flesh and blood. Rather, their spirit is taken upward and says to God, Turn away from this one.

Rabbi Meir would say: See, the verse says, "My spirit shall not judge," for the Holy Blessed One said: They have declared in this generation that God will not judge them, that there is no Judge in the world, for God has abandoned the world.

Rabbi Yehudah HaNasi would say: See, it says, "My spirit shall not judge," for the Holy Blessed One said: They did not institute a court for themselves on earth, so I will institute a court for them on High."

Avot D'Rabbi Natan - Chapter 33

Chapter 33

There were ten generations from Adam until Noah. And why was it necessary to bring all those people into the world? But this is to teach us that all those generations continued to anger God, and there was not one among them who walked in the ways of the Holy Blessed One until Abraham our forefather came along, and he walked in the ways of the Holy Blessed One, as it says, "Because Abraham heeded My call and kept My charge, My commandments, My rules, and My Torahs." But there is only one Torah! How could he have kept Torahs, plural? This teaches that the Holy Blessed One planted two inner voices in Abraham, like two wise men, who helped him understand, advised him, and taught him wisdom all night long, as it says, "I will bless the Eternal who has advised me. Even at night, the voices inside of me [lit., my kidneys] have admonished me." Moreover, Abraham our forefather would always give charity first, and only after would he execute justice, as it says, "For I have singled him out, in order that he command his children and his household after him, and they will keep the way of the Eternal, doing charity [lit., righteousness], and justice." Whenever two parties to a conflict would come before Abraham our forefather seeking justice and one would say about the other: He owes me money, Abraham our forefather would take his own money and give it to the claimant. Then he would say to them: Make your cases before me. So, they would argue their cases. When he found that it was actually the first one who owed the money, he would say: Take the money in your hand, and give it to your fellow. And if no one owed money, he would say: Split what you have, and go in peace. But

Avot D'Rabbi Natan - Chapter 33

King David did not do it like this. Rather, he executed justice first, and only afterward gave charity, as it says, "And David would execute justice and charity [lit., righteousness] for all of his people." Whenever two parties to a dispute came before King David and one would say: This one owes me money, he would say to them: Make your cases. So, they would argue their cases. Then, when one was found to be liable to the other, David would take out his own money and give it to him. If no one owed money, he would say to them: Split what you have and go in peace.

Abraham our forefather was tested with ten trials before the Holy Blessed One, and he emerged from each one complete.

They are as follows: Two when God said to him, "Go forth!" Two with his two sons. Two with his two wives. One with the war of the kings. One at the Covenant of the Parts. One in Ur Kasdim. One with circumcision. The Covenant of the Parts. And why so many? So that when Abraham our forefather comes to take his reward, the angels will say: More than us, more than anyone, Abraham deserves his reward, as it says, "Go, eat your bread with joy, and drink your wine with a happy heart."

Because Abraham was tested with ten trials, and emerged from each one complete, the Holy Blessed One performed ten miracles for his children in Egypt, and brought ten plagues, and performed ten more miracles at the sea, and brought ten more plagues upon the Egyptians at the sea.

The Egyptians roared at the top of their lungs, and so the Holy Blessed One thundered back across the sea, as it says, "God thunders marvellously with His voice." The Egyptians came to the sea with bows and arrows, and so

Avot D'Rabbi Natan - Chapter 33

the Holy Blessed One appeared before them with a bow and arrow, as it says, "Bared and ready is your bow," and, "He sent forth His arrows and scattered them...." The Egyptians came to the sea with swords, so the Holy Blessed One came upon them with swords and mercy, as it says, "He sent forth His arrows and scattered them; He discharged lightning and routed them." And lighting always means a sword, as it says, "The sword, the sword has been sharpened and polished, sharpened in order to slaughter, so that it sparkles like lightning." The Egyptians came proudly with shield and armour, and so the Holy Blessed One did the same, as it says, "Grab shield and armour and rise to my defense." The Egyptians came with spears, and so did the Holy Blessed One, as it says, "Your flashing spear in brilliance." The Egyptians came with rocks and slings, and the Holy Blessed One outdid them with hailstones, as it says, "Out of the brilliance before Him, hail and fiery coals pierced His clouds."

When our ancestors stood at the sea, Moses said to them: Arise and cross! They said to him: We will not cross until the sea begins to split open. So, Moses took his staff and struck the sea, and it began to split open, as it says, "You will split open the heads of his warriors with your staff." Moses said to them: Arise and cross! They said to him: We will not cross until the sea becomes like a valley before us. So, Moses struck the sea and it became like a valley before them, as it says, "He split the sea and passed them through," and, "Like a beast going down into the valley." Moses said to them: Arise and cross! They said: We will not cross until it is divided into sections, as it says, "Who divided the Sea of Reeds into sections." Moses said to them: Arise and cross! They said: We will

Avot D'Rabbi Natan - Chapter 33

not cross until it becomes solid matter. So, Moses took his staff and struck the sea, and it became mud, as it says, "You led your horse into the sea, onto solid waters." Moses said to them: Arise and cross! They said: We will not cross until it becomes a desert. So Moses took his staff and struck the sea, as it says, "He led them through the depths as if it were the desert." Moses said to them: Arise and cross! They said: We will not cross until it becomes all smashed up into particles. So, Moses took his staff and struck the sea, as it says, "You smashed the sea with your might." Moses said to them: Arise and cross! They said: We will not cross until it becomes a bed of rocks. He took his staff and struck the sea, as it says there, "You broke the heads of crocodiles on the water." And they could not be broken like this except on rocks. Moses said to them: Arise and cross! They said: We will not cross until it becomes dry land. So, Moses took his staff and struck the sea, as it says, "He turned the sea into dry land," and, "And the children of Israel walked on dry land in the midst of the sea." Moses said to them: Arise and cross! They said: We will not cross until it becomes walls. So, Moses took his staff and struck the sea, as it says, "And the water became a wall for them, on their right and on their left." Moses said to them: Arise and cross! They said: We will not cross until goatskins nodot to drink from appear before us. So, Moses took his staff and struck the sea, as it says, "The walls stood like a stack ned of flowing water." And where do we learn that between the sections, fire came down and, as it says, "Like fire kindles brushwood, and fire boils water to announce your name to your antagonists"? And so, the goatskins would draw oil and honey into the mouths of the babies, who would nurse from them, as it says, "He nursed him with honey

Avot D'Rabbi Natan - Chapter 33

from the rock." And some say that fresh water flowed from the sea, and they would drink it between the sections of the sea, since seawater is usually salty, for it says, "flowing," which always means sweet, as it says, "A well of fresh water, flowing from the Lebanon." And the Clouds of Glory were above them, so that the sun would not oppress them. And this is how the Israelites crossed the water, in order that they would feel no pain.

Rabbi Eliezer would say: The sea depths were arched over them from above, and the Israelites crossed through, so that they would feel no pain. Rabbi Elazar and Rabbi Shimon would say: The upper waters and the lower waters tossed the Egyptians, as it says, "The Eternal tossed the Egyptians into the sea."

Avot D'Rabbi Natan - Chapter 34

Chapter 34

The Holy Blessed One tested our ancestors with ten trials, and they did not emerge whole from any of them. They are as follows: "In the wilderness, on the plain, facing Suf, between Paran, and Tophel, and Lavan, and Hatzerot, and Di-zahav". "In the wilderness": When they made the Golden Calf, as it says, "They made themselves a molten calf." "On the plain": Because of water, as it says, "There the people thirsted for water." "Facing Suf": When they rebelled at the Sea of Reeds and some say: This was the idol that Micah made. Rabbi Yehudah said: They rebelled at the sea, meaning, they rebelled in the sea, as it says, "They rebelled at the Sea of Reeds." "Between Paran": With regard to the spies, "Moses sent them from the wilderness of Paran." "And Tophel": These were the frivolous words tiphlot they said about the manna. "Lavan": This was Korah's mutiny. "Hatzerot": Because of the quails. So far, that is seven. But in another place, it says, "At Tav'erah, and at Masah, and at Kivrot HaTa'avah." "Di-zahav": This is when Aaron said to them: Enough dai of this golden zahav sin which you have committed with the calf! But Rabbi Eliezer Ben Ya'akov would say: Terrible enough dai is this sin that Israel was punished for to last from now until the resurrection of the dead.

The Holy Blessed One is praised with ten names. They are as follows: A-D-O-N-A-I, E-L-O-H-I-M, E-L-O-A-H, E-L-O-H-E-Kh-A, E-L-O-H-E-Kh-E-M, E-L, E-H-I-Y-E-H A-S-H-E-R E-H-I-Y-E-H, Sh-A-D-A-I, and Tzevaot. Rabbi Yosei disagreed that Tzevaot was one of them, for it says, "Appoint generals for the armies tzevaot to head the people."

Avot D'Rabbi Natan - Chapter 34

Idol worship is denounced with ten names. They are as follows: shikutzim abominations, gilulim filth, maseichot molten figures, p'silim sculpted sigures, elilim false gods, asheirim tree idols, hamanim sun icons, atzavim forms, aven wickedness, and teraphim statues.

Two signs two Hebrew letters nun inverted are given in the Torah to mark off a small section. What is this section? "And when the Ark would travel…". Rabban Shimon ben Gamliel would say: It would be more appropriate take this section out from where it is, and have it written in a different place. There is a similar sign in the verse, "And Jonathan, son of Gershom, son of Menashe." Was Gershom the son of Menashe? No, he was the son of Moses. But his actions were not like those of Moses his father, so they added a nun to connect him to Menashe instead.

A similar exegesis was applied to the verse, "These are the two sons of the pure oil, who serve the Master of all the Earth." These are Aaron and the Messiah. I would not be able to tell which of them was the more beloved, except that it says with regard to the Messiah, "The Eternal has sworn and will not change His mind; you will be a priest forever, the rightful king that I have chosen". From this verse we know that the messianic king is even more beloved than a rightful priest.

See, it says, "A wild boar from the forest hazir miya'ar will gnaw at it." Shouldn't it say: A hippopotamus from the river hazir miye'or will gnaw at it? But it says "from the forest," because when Israel does not do the will of God, then the gentiles will come upon them like a wild boar from the forest. Just as a wild boar from the forest will kill people and injure other animals, and is a torment to people, so whenever Israel does not do the will of God,

Avot D'Rabbi Natan - Chapter 34

the gentiles will come and kill them, torture them, and injure them. But when Israel does the will of God, the gentiles do not rule over them, and are like a hippopotamus from the river. Just as a hippopotamus does not kill people, and causes no injury to other creatures, so whenever Israel does the will of God, no foreign nation will kill, injure, or torture them. And then it will be written as: From the river [i.e., miye'or, with an aleph, instead of miya'ar, with an ayin].

Ten words in the Torah are marked with dots. They are as follows: "The Eternal will judge between me and you". There is a dot above the letter yod in the term, "and you." This teaches that Sarah did not say this to Abraham, but to Hagar. Some say that it means she was speaking about those who caused the fighting "between me and you." "They said to him, where is Sarah?" There are dots above the letter's aleph, yod, and vav in the term, "to him," to indicate that they already knew where she was, but they nevertheless inquired about her. There is a dot on the verse, "When she lay down and when she arose". There is a dot above the letter vav in the term, "When she arose" the first time it is used with regard to Lot's older daughter. This teaches that he was not aware of what happened until the younger daughter arose. "And Esau ran to greet him, and he hugged him, fell on his neck, and kissed him". The term for, "and kissed him," has dots above every letter, to teach that he did not kiss him sincerely. Rabbi Shimon Ben Elazar would say: It means that this kiss was sincere, but every other one he gave Jacob was not. "His brothers went to shepherd their father's flocks in Shechem" There are dots on the word just before "flocks." This teaches that they did not actually go to shepherd the flocks, but to eat and drink and indulge their temptations. "Moses and

Avot D'Rabbi Natan - Chapter 34

Aaron recorded all the Levites. There are dots above Aaron's name. Why? To teach that Aaron himself was not counted in this record... "On a long journey". There is a dot above the letter hei in the word "long." This teaches that this does not really mean a long journey, but any exiting the boundaries of the outer court of the Temple. "We caused destruction all the way up to Nophach, which reaches into Medeba". There is a dot above the letter reish in the word "which." Why? In order to teach that they destroyed the idolaters but not the countries themselves, whereas the practice of idolaters was to destroy entire countries. "A tenth, a tenth for each". This verse delineates the meal offering that accompanies the burnt offering on the first day of the Sukkot festival. There is a dot above the letter vav in the first occurrence of the word "tenth." Why? To teach that there is only one-tenth measure for each. "The hidden things are for the Eternal our God and the revealed things are for us and our children forever". There are dots above the words "for us and our children and above the letter ayin in the word "forever." Why? For this is what Ezra said: If Elijah comes and says to me: Why did you write it this way? I will say to him: I have already put dots above these words to indicate I was not certain it was correct. But if he says to me: You wrote it correctly, and then I will remove the dots.

There are eleven instances in the Torah where the Hebrew word for "she," היא, is written as הוא which means "he" or "it" but vocalized to mean "she." The first is: "The King of Bela, he is [i.e., "she is"] Tzur". The second: "He himself said to me, 'She is my sister,' and SHE also said, 'He is my brother'. The third: "As she was being brought out, SHE sent a message to her father-in-law, saying".

Avot D'Rabbi Natan - Chapter 34

The fourth: "If one of your animals of which it is [i.e., "she is"] used for food dies". The fifth: "And it [i.e., "and she"] has turned the hair white". The sixth: "If the priest sees it…and it [i.e., "and she"] has faded". The seventh: "It [i.e., "she"] shall be a Sabbath of complete rest for you". The eighth: "And SHE sees his nakedness". The ninth: "SHE has disgraced her father". The tenth: "And SHE has kept secret, and defiled herself and she was not caught". The eleventh: "A spirit of jealousy has passed over him, and he is jealous of his wife…but SHE has not defiled herself".

The Divine Presence descended to the world ten times. Once in the Garden of Eden, as it says, "They heard the sound of the Eternal God moving in the garden," and it also says, "My beloved has gone down to his garden." Once in the generation of the Tower of Babel, as it says, "And the Eternal went down to see the city and the tower." Once in Sodom, as it says, "I will go down and I will see about the cries that have come up to me." Once in Egypt, as it says, "I have come down to save them from the hands of the Egyptians." Once at the sea, as it says, "And He bent the heavens and came down." Once at Sinai, as it says, "And the Eternal came down upon Mount Sinai" before all the people. Once in the Temple, as it says, "And the Eternal said to me, this gate must be kept closed and is never to be opened…because the Eternal, the God of Israel, has come through it." And once in a pillar of cloud, as it says," And the Eternal came down in a cloud." And once more in the future, in the days of Gog and Magog, as it's says, "He will set his feet down, on that day, upon the Mount of Olives."

The Divine Presence would depart from one place and go to another in ten movements: From the Ark's cover to a

Avot D'Rabbi Natan - Chapter 34

cherub; from a cherub to the threshold of the Temple; from the threshold to in between the two cherubs; from in between the two cherubs to the roof of the Sanctuary; from the roof of the Sanctuary to the wall of the outer court; from the wall of the outer court to the altar; from the altar to the city; from the city to the Temple Mount; from the Temple Mount into the desert. From the Ark's cover to a cherub, as it is written, "And He mounted a chariot and flew." From a cherub to the threshold of the Temple, as it is written, "And the presence of God went up from the cherub on which it had rested to the threshold of the Temple." From the threshold to between the two cherubs, as it is written, "And the presence of the Eternal went out from the threshold of the Temple and stopped above the cherubs." From in between the two cherubs to the roof of the Sanctuary, as it is written, "It is better to rest upon the corner of a roof." From the roof of the Sanctuary to the wall of the outer court, as it is written, "And behold, my Lord was standing on a wall measured by a plumb line." From the wall of the outer court to the altar, as it is written, "I saw my Lord standing by the altar." From the altar to the city, as it is written, "The voice of the Eternal calls to the city." From the city to the Mount, as it is written, "The Presence of the Eternal ascended from the midst of the city and stood upon the Mount." From the Mount into the desert, as it is written, "It is better to dwell in a desert land." And finally it departed upward, as it says, "I will go and return to my place."

Prophets are referred to by ten names. And they are: representative, faithful one, servant, emissary, seer, watchman, lookout, dreamer, prophet, man of God.

Avot D'Rabbi Natan - Chapter 34

The Holy Spirit is referred to by ten terms. And they are: Parable, Metaphor, Riddle, Speech, Saying, Splendor, Command, Burden, Prophecy, and Vision.

There are ten words for Happiness. And they are: sasson joy, simcha happiness, gila rejoicing, rina songfulness, ditza amusement, tzahala exuberance, aliza felicity, hedva delight, tiferet splendor, alitza cheer.

Ten entities are considered truly "alive." The Holy Blessed One, as it says, "The Eternal is truly God; He is a living God." The Torah is called a Living Torah, as it says, "It is a Tree of Life for those who hold fast to it, and all its supporters are happy." Israel is called Alive, as it says, "And you, who cling to the Eternal your God, you are all alive today." A righteous person is called Life, as it says, "The fruit of the righteous is the Tree of Life." The Garden of Eden is called Living, as it says, "I will walk before the Eternal in the land of the living." One of the trees in the Garden was called the Tree of Life, as it says, "and the Tree of Life in the midst of the Garden. The Land of Israel is called the Land of the Living, as it says, "I will place radiance in the land of the living." Jerusalem is called Living, as it says, "I will walk before the Eternal in the land of the living." Acts of kindness are called Life, as it says, "For your kindness is better than life; my lips will praise you." A wise person is called Life, as it says, "The Torah of the wise is the source of life." Water is called Living, as it says, "On that day, living waters will come forth from Jerusalem."

Avot D'Rabbi Natan - Chapter 35

Chapter 35

Ten miracles were performed for our ancestors in the Holy Temple: The sanctified meat never spoiled; no woman ever miscarried after smelling the sanctified meat; Ten miracles were performed for our ancestors in Jerusalem: no one was ever injured in Jerusalem; no one stumbled and fell in Jerusalem; the fires of the altar were never extinguished in Jerusalem; no building ever collapsed in Jerusalem; no one in Jerusalem ever said: I cannot find an oven to cook the Passover offering; no one in Jerusalem ever said: I cannot find an affordable bed to sleep in; no one in Jerusalem ever said: This place is too cramped for me to stay in.

A house in Jerusalem cannot contract ritual impurity of leprous marks. Nor can it be judged as a condemned city. Nor can one build ledges, balconies, or water channels in public spaces, because they create an enclosure for death and impurity. Nor, may a corpse be left there overnight. Nor may human bones be carried through the city. Nor may a stranger be given permanent residence there. Nor may graves be placed there, except for the graves of members of the House of David or the prophetess Hulda, which have been there from the days of the first prophets. And when they removed all the graves from the city, why were these not removed? They say there was a grotto there that would take all the impurities out into the Kedron River. One may not plant any plants there. Nor may one make a garden or an orchard there, aside from the rose gardens which have been there since the days of the first prophets. Nor may one raise geese or chickens there, let alone pigs. Nor may garbage heaps be established there, because of impurity. A stubborn and

Avot D'Rabbi Natan - Chapter 35

rebellious son cannot be judged there, said Rabbi Natan, for it says, "His father and mother shall grab him and take him to the elders of the city, to the gate of his place"; but this is not his city, nor his place. Houses sold there cannot include the land they are on. Houses cannot be sold as a permanent possession in the city after twelve months. Rent may not be collected there, except for the use of beds and mattresses. Rabbi Yehudah said: even rent for beds and mattresses was not collected.

What would they do with the skins of the sacrificed animals? They would give them to the owners of guest houses. Rabbi Shimon Ben Gamliel said: innkeepers were inside the city, and the owners of guest houses were outside. The innkeepers would buy sheepskins with fine wool for four or five sela and then sell them to the people of Jerusalem, and that is how these homeowners got rich. One verse says, "In one of your tribes". Another verse says, "In all of your tribes." "In one of your tribes" refers to Judah and Benjamin. "In all of your tribes" refers to Jerusalem, which belongs to all of Israel. And what was in the territory of Judah? The Temple Mount, Chambers of Stone, and the outer courts. And what was in the territory of Benjamin? The Temple itself, the Hallway, the Holy of Holies, and the triangular extension that went around the space where the altar was built. Benjamin merited to host God's Might, as it says, "And He rests upon his shoulders."

Rabbi Yehoshua Ben Levi said: When I know that that the Temple is going to be built again between the territories of Judah and Benjamin, I will go and prepare the fields of Jericho. And who ate the produce of those fields during all those years? The Kenites, the descendants of Moses' father-in-law, as says, "And the

Avot D'Rabbi Natan - Chapter 35

Kenites, the descendants of Moses' father-in-law, went up from the City of Palms."

He also said: When the Holy Blessed One removed His Presence, He promised to give a great reward in the future to Jethro and his descendants. How do we know that the descendants of Jethro were supported from charity in the meantime? Because of what it says, "The families of the tribes that dwelled at Jabez," and then, "They were the potters, who dwelled in the plantations." They were great men, owners of houses, fields, and vineyards. And because of the work of the King of all kings, the Holy Blessed One, they dwelled there in the king's service. So then where did they go? They went to Jabez to study Torah, and there they became a people of God. At that time Jabez was a good and righteous man, a man of truth and piety, and he would sit and teach Torah, as it says, "And Jabez called out to the God of Israel, saying if you bless me…and God granted his request."

Ten miracles were performed for our ancestors in the Holy Temple: Flies were never seen in the slaughterhouse. No high priest ever had an emission on Yom Kippur - except for Rabbi Yishmael Ben Kimkhit, who went out to speak with a certain official, and some saliva came out of the official's mouth and fell on the clothes of Rabbi Yishmael, and so his brother went in to serve as the high priest in his place. So, his mother was able to see two of her sons serve as the high priest on the same day. The sages saw her and asked her, "How did you merit this honor?" She replied, "Because the walls of my house never saw my hair uncovered." No one in Jerusalem was ever hurt, and no one was ever injured or stumbled and fell, in the Holy Temple. No woman ever miscarried after smelling the sanctified meat. The priests

Avot D'Rabbi Natan - Chapter 35

never disqualified the holy offerings. And when they ate the holy meat, they would drink from the waters of the Shiloach and it would digest in their stomachs like regular food.

There was never a defect in the Omer offering, or in the two loaves, or in the showbread.

A clay vessel that shattered would be immediately absorbed back into the ground. The wind never disturbed the pillar of cloud of incense. When the pillar of cloud came out of the altar, the smoke from the offering would shoot straight up like a staff until it reached the sky and when the smoke from the incense would come out of the golden altar, it would wind its way into the Holy of Holies.

Though people would stand tightly packed together, when they bowed there was plenty of space. For when Israel went up to worship their Father in heaven, when they sat down, they would be so crowded together that no one could fit a finger between them. But when they would bow, there was plenty of space.

But the greatest miracle of them all was that if even a hundred people bowed at the same time, the sexton of the congregation would never have to make an announcement telling people to make space for one another. Miracles were also performed in the courtyard, for even if all of Israel entered into the courtyard, it could contain them all. But an even greater miracle was that when all of Israel would stand so packed together during prayer that no one could fit a finger between them, when they would bow down, a space was created between each of them as wide as the height of a person.

Rabban Shimon Ben Gamliel would say: In the future, all the nations and all the kingdoms will gather together in

Avot D'Rabbi Natan - Chapter 35

Jerusalem, as it says, "And all the nations will assemble there in the name of the Eternal," and it says, "Let the waters be assembled." Just as there the assembly of all the waters in Creation were in one place, so too, the assembly here is a gathering of all the nations and kingdoms into Jerusalem, as it says, "And all the nations will assemble there."

Avot D'Rabbi Natan - Chapter 36

Chapter 36

The men of Sodom will not be granted eternal life, and will not even be given a trial, as it says, "And the men of Sodom were very wicked and sinful against the Eternal." "Wicked" – with one another; "and sinful" – through sexual transgression. "Against the Eternal", by desecrating God's name; "very" – for they were very intent on sinning. These are the words of Rabbi Akiva.

But Rabbi Yehoshua said: They will be given a trial! As it says, "Therefore the wicked will not survive judgment, nor will sinners, in the assembly of the righteous." That is, they will not stand in the assembly of the righteous, but they will stand in the assembly of the wicked. But Rabbi Nehemiah said: They will not make it to the assembly of the wicked. As it says, "May sinners disappear from the earth and the wicked be no more."

The minor children of the wicked will not be granted eternal life, and will not even be given a trial, as it says, "For behold, the day is coming that will burn like a furnace and all the arrogant and the doers of evil will be like straw, and when that day comes, says the Eternal, Master of Legions, it will burn them to ashes and leave no root or branch." These are the words of Rabbi Akiva.

But Rabbi Yehoshua said: They will be given a trial! It is about them that the verse says, "He called loudly and said, cut down the tree, chop off its branches, strip off its foliage, and scatter is fruit." And then it says, "But leave the stump with its roots in the ground in fetters of iron and bronze." Both the verses in Malachi and in Daniel mention roots. Just as the roots in the later passage refer to their bodies, so too do the roots in the earlier passage refer to the human body. If so, how do I interpret the

Avot D'Rabbi Natan - Chapter 36

words, "It will…leave no root or branch"? So that they will have no merit on which they can depend.

Others agree that they will be given a trial, but say that the verse which speaks of them is, "This one will say, I am for the Eternal! And that one will use the name Jacob; another one will write For the Eternal on his arm, and take on the name Israel. "This one will say, I am for the Eternal!" – Those are the totally righteous. "That one will use the name Jacob" – those are the minor children of the wicked. "Another one will write For the Eternal on his arm" – these are the wicked who cease their evil ways and repent and return to the good. "And take on the name Israel" – these are the converts from all the nations of the world.

Korah and his company will not be granted eternal life, and will not even be given a trial, as it says, "The earth closed over them, and they vanished from the midst of the congregation." These are the words of Rabbi Eliezer.

But Rabbi Yehoshua said: They will be given a trial! It is about them that the verses speak, "The Eternal deals death and gives life, casts down into Sheol and raises up." The verse that speaks of Sheol: "They went down alive into Sheol, with all that belonged to them." And the verse in I Samuel speaks of Sheol. So just as later one can be cast down into Sheol or raised up from it, so too, when Sheol is mentioned here, they go down into it, but will one day be raised up from it.

Rabbi Eliezer said: Then how do you interpret the verse, "The earth closed over them, and they vanished from the midst of the congregation"? Rabbi Yehoshua responded: They vanished from the midst of the congregation, but they did not vanish from the World to Come.

Avot D'Rabbi Natan - Chapter 36

The generation of the desert will not be granted eternal life, and will not even be given a trial, as it says, "In this very desert they will die, there they will perish." And it also says, "Those who I swore, in my anger, would never come to my resting place." These are the words of Rabbi Eliezer.

But Rabbi Yehoshua said: They will be given a trial! It is about them that the verses speak, "Gather to me my devotees, who made a covenant with me over sacrifice." Rabbi Eliezer said to him: Accept my interpretation. For if not, how can you explain the words, "Those who I swore, in my anger"? Rabbi Yehoshua replied: These are the spies, and all the wicked people of that generation.

Then Rabbi Yehoshua asked: So, what do you do with the verse, "Gather to me my devotees"? Rabbi Eliezer said to him: That refers to Moses and Aaron, and all the devotees of that generation from the Tribe of Levi.

Others responded above: How do you know the word "there" is referring only to the wicked, and not to the righteous? Didn't it already say, "There they buried Abraham, and Sarah his wife"? And it also says, "In my grave, which I prepared for myself in the land of Canaan, there shall you bury me." And it also says, "And Miriam died there, and was buried there." And what's more, "Aaron the priest went up…and died there." And it also says, "And Moses, the servant of the Eternal, died there in the land of Moab, by the word of the Eternal."

Rabbi Yosei HaGalili said: They will not be given a trial! For it says, "In this very desert they will die, there they will perish." And it also says, "There, by the stream, they shall break the calf's neck." Just as we have the word "there" in the case of the calf whose neck is broken, which dies and never leaves that place, so too, the word

Avot D'Rabbi Natan - Chapter 36

"there" in the case of those who died in the desert indicates that they will die and never leave that place.

And others say: They will be given a trial! It is about them that the verse speaks: "Go and call to the ears of Jerusalem and say... I will remember as a kindness the devotion of your youth."

Ten of the tribes will not be granted eternal life, and will not even be given a trial, for it says, "The Eternal plucked them up from the ground and cast them into another land, where they remain to this day." Rabbi Shimon Ben Yochai says: Just as "this day" on which they have rebelled passes and will never return, so will they never return. But Rabbi Akiva says: Just as "this day" is dark and then gets lighter, so will their darkness one day become lighter. Rabbi Gamliel says: See, it says, "In order that you and your children will endure." And it also says, "Parents shall not be put to death for their children." So, when the parent's life extends, so does the child's. But when the parent's life does not extent, neither does the child's. Rabbi Yosei HaGalili supports the position of Rabbi Eliezer, and Rabbi Gamliel supports the position of Rabbi Yehoshua.

These seven have no share in the World to Come: the scribe, the schoolteacher, the best doctors, the city judge, the magician, the sexton, and the butcher.

Three kings and four commoners have no share in the World to Come. The three kings are: Jeroboam, Ahab, and Menashe. The four commoners are: Bil'am, Doeg, Ahitophel, and Gehazi. Rabbi Yehudah would say: Menashe already repented, as it says, "And he prayed to God, and God granted his prayer…." They replied: If that verse had continued only with, "…and returned him to Jerusalem," and stopped, we would have said exactly

Avot D'Rabbi Natan - Chapter 36

what you said. But because it continues and says, "…and to his kingship," that means he was returned to his kingdom and not returned to the World to Come.

Rabbi Meir would say: Absalom has no share in the World to Come. Rabbi Yohanan Ben Guri said: Even one who pronounces God's name as it is written has no share in the World to Come. He would also say: One who sings Song of Songs with a vibrato has no share in the World to Come. One who whispers incantations over a wound, one who spits into a wound, or chants over a wound, "I will no longer afflict you with all the diseases that I put upon you in Egypt," does not have a share in the World to Come.

The sages would say: Any Torah scholar who stops learning has no share in the World to Come, as it says, "Because he has spurned the word of the Eternal." And it also says, "What wrong did your ancestors find in me that caused them to distance themselves from Me?"

Rabbi Meir would say: Anyone who has a study hall in his city and never goes there has no share in the World to Come. Rabbi Akiva would say: Even someone who does not serve the scholars has no share in the World to Come.

Avot D'Rabbi Natan - Chapter 37

Chapter 37

Seven things were created, and each one was greater than the next. God created the sky, which was then the greatest thing of all. Then God created the stars, which were even greater, for they could illuminate the world. Then God created the trees, which were even greater, for they produced fruit, which the stars could not do. Then God created the wicked winds, which were even greater, for they could go from place to place, while the trees could not move from where they were planted. Then God created the animal, which was even greater, for the animal could make things and eat, which the wicked winds could not. Then God created the human being, which was even greater, for the human being had the capacity for knowledge, which the animal did not. Then God created the angels who serve God, who were even greater, for they could move from one end of the world to the other, which the human being could not do.

Six things can be said of human beings, three ways in which they are like animals and three ways in which they are like the angels who serve God. The three ways they are like animals: They eat and drink like animals, they reproduce like animals, and they excrete like animals. And the three ways they are like angels who serve God: They have understanding like the angels who serve God, they walk upright like the angels who serve God, and they speak in the holy tongue [i.e., Hebrew] like the angels who serve God.

Six things can be said of demons, three ways in which they are like human beings and three ways in which they are like the angels who serve God. The three ways they are like human beings: They eat and drink like human

Avot D'Rabbi Natan - Chapter 37

beings, they reproduce like human beings, and they die like human beings. And the three ways they are like angels who serve God: They have wings like the angels who serve God, they know what will happen in the future like the angels who serve God, and they can move from one end of the world to the other like the angels who serve God. And some say that they can also change their faces into any form they wish, and that they can see but are themselves unseen.

There are seven types of false Pharisees: the Shechemite Pharisee, the Nakfaite Pharisee, the Miktzoite Pharisee, the Machobaite Pharisee, the Pharisee for the sake of a profession, the Pharisee who was obligated by marriage, the Pharisee driven by lust, and the Pharisee driven by fear.

Eight things are hard on a person when done excessively, but pleasant if done sparingly: drinking wine, work, sleep, having wealth, sexual relations, bathing in hot water, sexual relations, and bloodletting.

The Holy Blessed One created the world with seven things: with knowledge, with understanding, with might, with rebuke, with judgment, with kindness, and with mercy.

And just as He created the world with seven things, so too did He create these seven: the three patriarchs and the four matriarchs.

Seven attributes serve before the Throne of Glory: Wisdom, Righteousness, Justice, Kindness, Mercy, Truth, and Peace, as it says, "I will bind you to me forever. I will bind you to me with righteousness, with justice, with kindness, and with mercy. I will bind you to me with faith, and you will know the Eternal." Rabbi Meir would say: What do we learn from the phrase, "and

Avot D'Rabbi Natan - Chapter 37

you will know the Eternal"? This teaches that any person who possesses these attributes has knowledge of God.

There are seven realms: the upper realm, the lower realm, the air of the world, and the four upper areas. Rabbi Meir says: There are seven skies: Vilon, Rakia, Shekhakim, Zevul, Ma'on, Machon, and Aravot. The land, likewise, is called by seven names: Eretz, Adama, Arka, Haravah, Yabasha, Tevel, and Heled. And why is it called Tevel? Because it is seasoned metubelet with everything. Another interpretation: Because its nature is to bring in and not to take out.

There are seven distinctions between one righteous person and another: One has a more pleasant wife than the other; one has more pleasant children than the other; both eat from one bowl, but this one tastes according to what he has done and that one tastes according to what he has done; both of them dye cloth with the same kettle, but this one's comes out lovely and that one's comes out ugly; one's wisdom is greater; one's understanding is greater; and one's knowledge is greater and one is taller, as it says , "The greater one guides the righteous."

Hillel the Elder presented seven interpretive principles before the House of Beteira: kal vahomer an a fortiori inference: if so for a lenient case, all the more so for a stringent case, gezeira shava similar principle learned from linking words, binyan av building on a primary category, miklal u'frat specific cases limiting the general rule, miprat u'klal a generalization expanding the application of a specific case, kayotzei bo bemakom akher a similar case in another place, and davar halamed minyano a principle learned out from context; these are the seven interpretive principles that Hillel the Elder presented before the House of Beteira.

Avot D'Rabbi Natan - Chapter 37

A fool has seven traits and a wise person has seven traits: When a wise person does not understand, he says: I do not understand. He does not become embarrassed, but simply admits to what is true. And all the opposite things are said about the fool.

The wise person does not speak before one who is greater than him in wisdom.

From whom do we learn this? From Moses, as it says, "Aaron repeated all the words that the Eternal had spoken to Moses, and he performed the signs in the sight of the people." And who was the appropriate person to say all these things, Moses or Aaron? One would assume Moses, for Moses had heard them from the mouth of the Almighty, whereas Aaron had heard them just from Moses! However, Moses said to himself: Can I speak in place of my older brother while he is standing right there? Therefore, he told Aaron to speak, as it says, "Aaron repeated all the words that the Eternal had spoken to Moses."

And he does not interrupt his fellow.

This is Aaron as it says, "Then Aaron spoke…see, this day they brought their sin offering and their burnt offering." But he was quiet until Moses had finished speaking, and he did not tell Moses to cut his words short. Only afterward did he say to Moses, "See, this day they brought their sin offering and their burnt offering," but we are in mourning and cannot eat of the offerings. And some say that Aaron pulled Moses aside and said to him, "Moses my brother, tithes are the least important of the offerings, and it is still forbidden for a mourner to eat them. A sin offering is the most important of the offerings, so all the more so is it forbidden for a mourner to eat it! Immediately, Moses admitted that Aaron was

Avot D'Rabbi Natan - Chapter 37

right, as it says, "And when Moses heard this, it was good in his eyes." And in the eyes of the Almighty.

We learn also from the fact that Moses became angry with Elazar and Itamar, Aaron's sons. From this, they say that when a person makes a celebration for his students, he turns his attention to the greatest of them. But when he becomes angry with them, he directs his anger to the lowliest among them, as it says, "And he became angry with Elazar and Itamar." This shows that he was actually angry with Aaron as well.

Aaron was older than Moses, but the Eternal is greater than Aaron! So why didn't the Eternal speak to Aaron? Because he did not have his sons stand guard. Because if he had put Elazar and Itamar on guard, then he could have kept Nadav and Avihu from sinning.

We learn also from Abraham our forefather, who prayed for the men of Sodom. The Holy Blessed One said to him, "If I find fifty righteous people in Sodom, I will save the whole place for their sake." But the One who spoke and brought the world into being already knew full well that if there were even three or five righteous people in Sodom, it would have been saved. Yet the Holy Blessed One waited until Abraham finished talking, and only afterward replied, as it says, "When the Eternal had finished speaking to Abraham, He departed…"As if the Eternal had said to Abraham, see, now I am released, as it says at the end of the verse, "…and Abraham returned to his place."

And he does not become agitated and respond too quickly.

This is Elihu Ben Berakhel HaBuzi, as it says, "I said to myself: Let age speak first." This teaches that they were sitting in silence before Job. When he would stand up,

Avot D'Rabbi Natan - Chapter 37

they would stand up. When he would sit down again, they would sit down again. When he ate, they would eat. When he drank, they would drink. Finally, he asked permission to speak, as it says, "Afterward, Job began to speak, and cursed the day of his birth." And he said, "Perish the day on which I was born, and the night it was announced: A male has been conceived!" Perish the day that my father came to my mother and she told him: I am pregnant. And how do we know that they did not all start speaking at the same time? For it says, "Job answered and said…" and then, "Elifaz HaTeimani answered and said…" and then, "Bildad HaShukhi answered and said…" and then, "Tzofar HaNa'amati answered and said…" and then, "Elihu ben Berakhel HaBuzi answered and said…." The book lays them out one at a time however, to let everyone know that a wise person does not speak before someone who is greater in wisdom. And a person does not interrupt his fellow. And does not become agitated and respond quickly.

He asks appropriately. This is Judah, as it says, "I will pledge myself for him."

He asks inappropriately. This is Reuben, as it's says, "Reuben said to his father: Let my two sons die!"

He speaks of first things first. This is Jacob. And some say this is Sarah.

And last things last. These are the men of Haran.

And he admits to what is true. This is Moses, as it says, "The Eternal said to me…they did well to speak thus." So, too, did the Holy Blessed One admit to what was true, as it says, "The daughters of Tzelophechad have spoken correctly."

Avot D'Rabbi Natan - Chapter 38

Chapter 38

Seven types of punishments come into the world, due to seven kinds of sin.

When some tithe and some do not, famine comes because of drought. When some donate to the priesthood and some do not, famine comes because of chaos. When some separate the dough offering challah and some do not, famine comes because of devastation. When no one tithes, they stop up the heavens from giving dew and rain, and people toil and toil and never have enough. Rabbi Yoshia said: For the sin of not separating the dough offering, fruit are not blessed, and people toil and toil and never have enough. For the sin of not donating to the priesthood or tithing, the heavens are stopped up, and do not give any dew or rain, and the people are given over to the hands of their enemies.

Pestilence comes into the world because of the sins of not leaving aside in one's field during the harvest the dropped produce, the forgotten produce, the corner of the field, and the tithe for the poor. There is a story of a woman who was sitting in the neighborhood of a field owner. Her two sons had gone out to collect the left produce, but the field owner had not left it. The mother said: When will my sons come back from the field? Perhaps they will bring me a bit to eat. And her sons said: Shall we go to see our mother? Perhaps she will have a bit for us to eat. But they had nothing for her, and she had nothing for them. The sons laid their heads on their mother's knees, and all three of them died that day. The Holy Blessed One said: You have taken their lives, so I, too, will take your lives! And this is what is meant by the verses, "Do not rob from the wretched, because he is wretched. Do not

Avot D'Rabbi Natan - Chapter 38

crush the poor man at the gate. For the Eternal will take up their cause, and despoil those who despoil them of life."

The sword comes into the world because of the delay and perversion of justice, and because of those who teach the Torah contrary to the Halakhah. When Rabbi Shimon Ben Gamliel and Rabbi Yishmael were taken out to be killed, Rabbi Shimon Ben Gamliel was sitting and wondering, and he said: Woe are we, for we are being killed like those who violate the Sabbath, worship idols, commit sexual transgressions, and murder! Rabbi Yishmael Ben Elisha said: May I suggest something to you? Rabbi Shimon said: Go ahead. Rabbi Yishmael said: Perhaps you were once sitting at a meal, and some poor people came and stood at your door, and you did not allow them to come in to eat? Rabbi Shimon said: Heaven forbid I ever did something like that! I had guards posted at my door, so that when poor people came, they would be let in to sit and drink with me, and then bless the heavenly Name with me. So, Rabbi Yishmael said: Perhaps when you were sitting and preaching on the Temple Mount, and all of Israel were sitting before you, you became arrogant for a moment? Rabbi Shimon said: Yishmael my brother, a person must simply be ready to receive his punishment. So they went and pleaded with the executioner. One said: I am a priest, the son of a high priest. Kill me first, so that I do not have to witness the death of my friend. The other said: I am the leader of the community, the son of a former leader of the community. Kill me first, so that I do not have to witness the death of my friend. The executioner replied: Let's draw lots. So, they drew lots, and it fell on Rabbi Shimon. Immediately, the executioner took his sword and chopped off Rabbi

Avot D'Rabbi Natan - Chapter 38

Shimon's head. Rabbi Yishmael took it and held it to his chest and cried and shouted out: This holy mouth, this faithful mouth! This holy mouth, this faithful mouth! This mouth that brought forth precious jewels and gems and pearls! Who has buried you in the dirt? Who has stuffed your mouth with dirt and dust? Of you the verse speaks: "Arise, sword, against my shepherd, against my own beloved man!" He had not finished speaking when the sword came down and chopped off his head as well. About them the verse says: "My anger will rage, and I will kill them by the sword! And your wives will become widows, and your children will become orphans." From the fact that it says, "I will kill them by the sword," don't I know that their wives were made widows and their children were made orphans? But they both were and were not widows. For there were no witnesses there to testify, that these women were permitted to marry again. This is like what happened in Beitar, where not a soul survived to testify that a woman could marry again. And from the fact that it says, "your wives will become widows," don't I know that the children will be orphans? But they both were and were not orphans. For their inheritance stood in their fathers' name and was not given to them to inherit so they could marry and give it to their wives.

Exile comes into the world because of idolatry, sexual transgression, murder, and not letting the land rest during the sabbatical year. Idolatry, as it says, "I will destroy your altars." The Holy Blessed One said: Since you want to worship idols, I will exile you to a place where they worship idols. That is why it says, "I will destroy your altars." Not letting the land rest during the sabbatical year, as it says, "Then shall the land make up for its

Avot D'Rabbi Natan - Chapter 38

sabbatical years throughout all the time that it is desolate and you are in the land of your enemies." The Holy Blessed One said to them: Since you do not let the land rest, it will rest by itself and the number of months that you did not let it rest, it will rest by itself. That is why it says, "Then shall the land make up…all the time." sexual transgression: How so? Rabbi Yishmael son of Rabbi Yosei said: As long as Israel commits sexual transgressions, the Divine Presence removes itself from them, as it says, "Let no unseemly [lit., naked] thing be seen among you, so that God will turn away from you."

Avot D'Rabbi Natan - Chapter 39

Chapter 39

Five kinds of people cannot be forgiven: One, who constantly again and again sins; one who sins in a righteous generation. One who sins with the intent to repent? Anyone whose sins publicly desecrates God's name. A human being is incapable of grasping God's likeness. But if not for his sin, they would give him the keys, and he would know how heaven and earth were created. He would also say: Everything is planned. Everything is revealed. Everything is knowable. He would also say: Everything is given in trust, and a net is spread out over all living things. Repentance delays the judgment of the wicked, though their fate is already sealed. But the contentedness of the wicked ends badly. Power buries those who wield it. Repentance is suspended until Yom Kippur atones. Death along with repentance wipes clean. The wicked are paid, but the righteous accrue credit. The wicked are paid in this world – that is, the people who act as if they follow the Torah, but they have evil intentions, and there was never any good in them. The righteous accrue credit – that is, people who follow the Torah with good intentions, and there was never any bad in them. Both types receive just a little in this world, but for the righteous, a large remainder is accounted to them for the future. He would also say: Everyone leaves this world naked; if only one's leaving the world can be like one's coming into the world!

Rabbi Meir would say: Beloved is the human being, who was created in the image of God, as it says, "For in God's image did God make the human." Beloved are Israel, who are called children of the Omnipresent God, as it says, "You are children of the Eternal your God." Beloved are

Avot D'Rabbi Natan - Chapter 39

Israel, for they were given a valuable tool. With it the world was created, as it says, "For I have given you a good thing; do not forsake My Torah."

Rabbi Eliezer Bar Tzadok would say: What are the righteous like in this world? Like a tree that is planted in a pure place, but its branches extend out to an impure place. What do people say? Cut off that tree's branches so that all of it will be pure, as it should be. What are the wicked like in this world? Like a tree that is planted in an impure place, but its branches extend out to a pure place. What do people say? Cut off that tree's branches so that all of it will be impure, as it should be.

The lion has six names: Aryeh, Kefir, Lavi, Layish, Shakhal, and Shakhatz.

The snake has six names: Nahash, Saraf, Tanin, Tzifoni, Efeh, and Akhshuv.

Solomon had six names: Shlomo, Yedidya, Kohelet, Ben Yakeh, Agur, and Lemuel.

Avot D'Rabbi Natan - Chapter 40

Chapter 40

For four things a person reaps the benefit in this world, and the principal reward remains in the World to Come. They are: respect for parents, acts of kindness, bringing peace between two people, and the study of Torah which is equal to them all. For four things a person suffers the consequences in both this world and the World to Come. They are: idolatry, sexual transgression, murder, and evil speech which is the worst of them all.

A good deed takes root and yields fruit, as it says, "Say that the righteous is good, for he shall eat the fruit of his deeds." A sin takes root but yields no fruit, as it says, "Woe to the evil wicked one, for what his hands have produced, will be done to him." And some say: Sins do yield fruit, as it says, "They shall eat the fruit of their ways, and have their fill of their own counsels."

Anyone who causes others to do good, his own sins will not overtake him. For it cannot be that his students will inherit the World to Come while he himself goes down to Sheol, as it says, "For you will not abandon me to Sheol." And anyone who causes others to sin, no amount of repentance will ever help him. For it cannot be that his students go down to Sheol while he himself inherits the World to Come, as it says, "A person with blood on his hands will go down into a pit."

One who says: I will sin, and then I will repent, will not be given the opportunity to repent. If he says: I will sin and Yom Kippur will atone for me, then Yom Kippur will not atone for him. If he says: I will sin and my death will wipe my slate clean, then his death with not wipe his slate clean.

Rabbi Elazar son of Rabbi Yosei would say: One who

Avot D'Rabbi Natan - Chapter 40

sins, and then repents and returns to his uprightness, nevertheless remains in a state of sin until he is forgiven. One who says: I will sin and then I will repent, can be forgiven up to three times for this, but no more.

There are four types of people. The one who says: What's mine is yours, and what's yours is mine, etc.

There are four types of students: One who wants to learn and to teach others, he is looked on favorably. One who wants to learn but not to teach others, he is looked on unfavorably. One who wants to teach others but not to learn, he has a mediocre character and some say he has the character of someone from Sodom. One who wants neither to learn nor to teach others, this is a completely wicked person.

There are four types of people in the study hall: One who approaches others and sits down with them to learn, he has share in the learning. One who approaches others but does not sit down with them, he has no share in the learning. One who keeps his distance from others but still sits down with them to learn, he has share in the learning. One who keeps his distance from others and likewise, does not sit down with them, he has no share in the learning.

One who asks and answers questions has a share in the learning. One who sits and is quiet has no share in the learning. One who approaches others and sits down with them in order to listen and learn has a share in the learning. One who approaches others and sits down with them, but only so people will say: That man sits and learns from the sages, he has no share in the learning. One who keeps his distance in order to be respectful of those who are greater than him, but still sits down to learn, has a share in the learning. One who keeps his distance and

Avot D'Rabbi Natan - Chapter 40

sits to learn, but only so people will say: That man does not need a sage; he has no share in the learning. One who sits and asks questions, but only so people will say: That man sits before the sages; he has no share in the learning. One who sits and asks questions so that he may listen and learn, he has a share in the learning. One who sits and is quiet in order to listen and learn, he has a share in the learning. One who sits and is quiet, but only so people will say: That man sits quietly before the sages; he has no share in the learning.

There are four types of people who sit before the sages. There is one who is like a sponge, one who is like a sifter, one who is like a funnel, and one who is like a sieve. Who is like a sponge? This is the wise student who sits before the sages and learns Tanakh, Mishnah, Midrash, Halakhah, and Aggadah, and just like a sponge absorbs everything, this student absorbs everything. Who is like a sifter? This is the wise and alert student who sits before the sages and listens to them speak about Tanakh, Mishnah, Midrash, Halakhah, and Aggadah, and just like a sifter removes the coarse flour and gathers the fine flour, he lets go of what is useless and gathers what is valuable. Who is like a funnel? This is the stupid student, who sits before the scholars and listens to them speak about Tanakh, Mishnah, Midrash, Halakhah, and Aggadah, and just like a funnel takes something from here and lets it out there, so it is with everything that enters this students ears; it goes in one ear and out the other, one by one, until he has forgotten everything. Who is like a sieve? This is the wicked student, who sits before a sage and listens to Tanakh, Mishnah, Midrash, Halakhah, and Aggadah, and just like the sieve lets out the wine and holds onto the sediment, this student lets go

Avot D'Rabbi Natan - Chapter 40

of what is valuable and gathers what is useless.

They called Rabbi Eliezer Ben Ya'akov a punctured, shortened horn. Shortened how? This is like a baby who is given a pearl, and then given a piece of bread. He throws away the pearl and takes the bread. Then he is given some pottery, and he throws away the bread and takes the pottery and finds that he is holding nothing but an empty pot in his hands.

Rabban Gamliel the Elder spoke about four kinds of students: the impure fish, the pure fish, the fish from the Jordan, the fish from the Great Sea. What is the impure fish? A child of the poor, who has learned Tanakh, Mishnah, Midrash, Halakhah, and Aggadah, but has no knowledge, what is the pure fish? A child of the rich, who has learned Tanakh, Mishnah, Midrash, Halakhah, and Aggadah, and has knowledge, what is the fish from the Jordan? It is a scholar who has learned Tanakh, Mishnah, Midrash, Halakhah, and Aggadah, but does not know how to comment upon it. What is the fish from the Great Sea? It is a scholar who has learned Tanakh, Mishnah, Midrash, Halakhah, and Aggadah, and knows how to comment upon it.

There are four types of afflictions: the one that sees and is seen, the one that is seen but does not see, the one that sees but does not see, and the one that does not see and is not seen. What sees and is seen? The wolf, the lion, the tiger, the hyena, the snake, robbers, and conscription officers – these all see and are seen. What is seen but does not see? The sword, the bow, the spear, the knife, the staff, and rods – these are all seen but do not see. The affliction of the Evil Spirit sees but is not seen. The affliction of intestinal illness is not seen and does not see. There are four sages who appear in dreams. One who sees

Avot D'Rabbi Natan - Chapter 40

Rabbi Yohanan Ben Nuri in a dream should expect to acquire a fear of sin. One who sees Rabbi Elazar Ben Azariah should expect greatness and riches. One who sees Rabbi Yishmael should expect to receive wisdom. One who sees Rabbi Yishmael should worry about punishments.

There are three Torah scholars who appear in dreams. One who sees Ben Azzai in a dream should expect to acquire piety. One who sees Ben Zoma in a dream should expect to receive wisdom. One who sees Elisha Ben Abuya in a dream should worry about punishments.

There are three books of the Prophets that appear in dreams. One who sees the book of Kings in a dream should expect greatness and riches. One who sees the book of Isaiah in a dream should expect to receive comfort. One who sees the book of Jeremiah in a dream should worry about punishments.

There are three books from the Writings that appear in dreams. One who sees the book of Psalms in a dream should expect to acquire humility. One who sees the book of Proverbs in a dream should expect to acquire wisdom. One who sees the book of Job in a dream should worry about punishments.

Death for the wicked is beneficial for them and beneficial for the world. Death for the righteous is bad for them and bad for the world. Quiet for the wicked is bad for them and bad for the world. Quiet for the righteous is good for them and good for the world.

A person should not stand naked in front of the place of the Holy of Holies.

One who enters the bathroom should not turn toward the east or the west, but only to the sides, and should not relieve himself while standing, but only while sitting. A

Avot D'Rabbi Natan - Chapter 40

person should not wipe himself with his right hand, but only with his left. And why do they say a person should not wipe himself with his right hand, but only with his left? Rabbi Eliezer says: Because the right hand is used to point to words of Torah. Rabbi Yehoshua says: Because one eats and drinks with the right hand.

Any love that is dependent on something, when that thing perishes, the love perishes. What is an example of love that is dependent on something? The love of Amnon for Tamar.

Any debate that is carried out for the sake of Heaven is destined to endure. What is an example of a debate that is carried out for the sake of Heaven? The debate between Hillel and Shammai.

Any gathering that is for the sake of performing the commandment. What is an example of a gathering that is for the sake of performing the commandments? The Men of the Great Assembly. What is an example of a gathering that is not for the sake of performing the commandments? The assembly of the men of the Generation of the Dispersal those who built the Tower of Babel.

Avot D'Rabbi Natan - Chapter 41

Chapter 41

Rabbi Shimon would say: There are three crowns: the crown of Torah, the crown of priesthood, the crown of kingship – and the crown of a good name is the greater than all of them.

How does the crown of priesthood work? Even if someone paid all the silver and gold in the world, we could not give him the crown of priesthood, as it says, "It will be for him and his descendants after him an eternal covenant of priesthood." For the crown of kingship as well; even if someone paid all silver and gold in the world, we could not give him the crown of kingship, as it says, "My servant David shall be their prince for all time." But the crown of Torah is different. For anyone who wishes to partake in the work of Torah may come and partake, as it says, "Ho, all who are thirsty, go to the water!" That is, go and labor in words of Torah and do not occupy yourself with meaningless things.

There is a story of Rabbi Shimon Ben Yochai: He would regularly go and visit the sick. He once came upon somebody who was bloated due to intestinal illness, and was cursing God. Rabbi Shimon said: Empty one! You ought to be begging for mercy, and instead you are cursing? The man replied: The Holy Blessed One has departed from me and rested on you. And then he said: The Holy Blessed One has done properly by me, for I have left aside words of Torah and occupied myself with meaningless things.

There is a story of Rabbi Shimon Ben Elazar: He was once coming from Migdal Eder, from his teacher's house, and he was riding on a donkey. He was traveling along the coast, and he spotted somebody who was quite ugly.

Avot D'Rabbi Natan - Chapter 41

He said: Empty one, how ugly you are! Are all the people in your city as ugly as you? The man replied: What can I do about it? Go to the Artisan who made me and say to Him, how ugly is this vessel You made! When Rabbi Shimon realized that he had sinned, he got off his donkey and prostrated himself before the man. And he said: I have sinned against you. Forgive me. But the man replied: I will not forgive you until you go to the Artisan who made me and say, how ugly is this vessel You made! Rabbi Shimon followed after him for three mil. All the people in the city came out to greet him, and then said: Peace be upon you, Rabbi! The man said: Whom are you calling Rabbi? They said: The one who is traveling behind you. He said to them: If that is a rabbi, may there be no more like him in Israel! They said to him: God forbid! What did he do to you? He told them: Such-and-such he did to me. They said to him: Even so, forgive him! He said: I hereby forgive him, but only if he does not continue doing this. On that day, Rabbi Shimon went to his great study hall and taught: A person should always be soft like a reed, and not rigid like a cedar. For the reed, when all the winds come and blow against it, moves in their direction. But when the winds quiet down, the reed returns to its place. That is why the reed merited to be made into a quill that is used to write a Torah scroll. But the cedar does not stay in its place; when the southern wind comes and blows against it, it uproots the tree and flips it over. And then what happens to the cedar? Woodcutters come along and chop it up, and take from it to build houses and then throw the rest into the fire. And that is why they say: A person should always be soft like a reed, and not rigid like a cedar.

Avot D'Rabbi Natan - Chapter 41

Three things are said about people who give: One who gives charity will have blessing come upon him. One who gives a loan is even better. And one who lets someone else work with him so he can split his earnings is the best of them all.

There are three types of Torah scholars: The one who asks and answers questions is wise. The one who asks questions but does not answer them is a level below. And the one who does not ask and does not answer is at the lowest level.

Three kinds of sweat are good for the body: the sweat generated during illness, the sweat generated at the bathhouse, and the sweat from work. The sweat generated during illness is healing, but there is nothing like the sweat at the bathhouse.

There are six kinds of tears; three are good and three are bad. The good: tears of sadness, tears from smoke, and tears in the bathroom. The bad: tears from poison, tears from laughter, and tears from pungent fruit.

A clay vessel has three properties: it absorbs, it does not emit what it has absorbed, and it does not cause its contents to rot. A glass vessel has three properties: it does not absorb, it does not emit, and it maintains the condition of whatever inside of it; what is hot stays hot, what is cold stays cold.

Four situations make for bad sexual relations: when someone has just come off the road, when someone has just gotten up from learning, when someone has just gotten up from an illness, and when someone has just gotten out of prison.

Anyone who accepts upon himself four things will be accepted into the fellowship: that he will not go into a cemetery, that he will not raise lean animals, that he will

Avot D'Rabbi Natan - Chapter 41

not give a donation to an ignorant priest, that he will not deal with ritually pure items in the presence of an ignorant person, and that he will commit to eating chulin in the state of purity.

The money taken from Egypt was returned to its proper place, as it says, "They stripped the Egyptians." And it also says, "Joseph gathered in all the money." And it also says, "In the fifth year of King Rehoboam, King Shishak of Egypt marched against Jerusalem and carried off the treasures of the House of the Eternal." The heavenly writing was also returned to its place, as it says, "It flies from your eyes and is there no more, it grows wings and flies like an eagle, heavenward."

Rabbi Yehudah Ben Teima would say: Be strong like a leopard, light like an eagle, fast like a deer, and brave like a lion in doing the will of your Father in heaven.

He would also say: Love be beloved from the heavens, and study all the commandments.

If you've done your friend just a little bit of harm, think of it as a lot. And if you've done your friend a lot of good, think of it as a little. If your friend has done you just a little bit of good, think of it as a lot. And if he has done you a lot of harm, think of it as a little.

The "sponge" and the "sealed bottle" – these are types of Torah scholars. The "funnel" and the "tube" – these are types of scoundrels.

Be like a bottle that has no opening that air can get into. Learn how to accept pain. And forgive all offenses done to you.

These are the things that were made and then hidden: The Tent of Meeting, and the items inside it; the Ark and the broken tablets; the jar of manna; the rod of Moses; the flask of anointing oil; the staff of Aaron, with its almonds

Avot D'Rabbi Natan - Chapter 41

and flowers; the priestly garments and garments of the high priest. But the mortar and pestle of the House of Avtinus, the table, the lamp, the curtain, and the headband of the high priest – those are still kept in Rome.

There is a story of Rabbi Tarfon: He was sitting and teaching his students when a bride passed before him. He told her to stop. He brought her into his house and told his mother and his wife: Bathe her, oil her skin, put makeup on her, and dance before her until she reaches her husband's house.

These people decreed the sages have no share in the World to Come: Five kings and six commoners who sought greatness: Cain, Korah, Bil'am, Ahitophel, Doeg, and Gehazi.

Rabbi Yosei would say: The completely righteous are not included in this reckoning, nor are the completely wicked. Who, then, are we wondering about? All those in the middle. As it says, "Please, Lord, save my soul" – from the punishments of Gehenna, lest I be among those who go down into it screaming and come up from it screaming, as it says, "I will bring the third into the fire, and I will smelt them as one smelts silver, and test them as one tests gold." The House of Hillel say: As it says, "Your kindness is better than life itself, my lips praise you!" And it also says, "Take pity on me and them, in your abundant kindness" so that they are saved from the punishments of Gehenna.

Everything that the Holy Blessed One created in the world was created only for His glory, as it says, "All that has been called by my name, whom I have created, formed, and made for my glory." And it also says, "The Eternal will reign forever and ever."

Avot D'Rabbi Natan - Chapter 41

Rabbi Hananya Ben Akashya said: The Holy Blessed One wanted to give merit to Israel. Therefore, He increased the amount of Torah and mitzvot, as it says, "The Eternal desires, for the sake of His servant's righteousness, to expand and enhance the Torah."

Avot D'Rabbi Natan - Chapter 41

www.ingramcontent.com/pod-product-compliance
Lightning Source LLC
Chambersburg PA
CBHW070139080526
44586CB00015B/1762